Arthur Cushman McGiffert

Dialogue Between a Christian and A Jew

Arthur Cushman McGiffert

Dialogue Between a Christian and A Jew

ISBN/EAN: 9783337136444

Printed in Europe, USA, Canada, Australia, Japan

Cover: Foto ©ninafisch / pixelio.de

More available books at **www.hansebooks.com**

DIALOGUE

BETWEEN

A CHRISTIAN AND A JEW

ENTITLED

ΑΝΤΙΒΟΛΗ ΠΑΠΙΣΚΟΥ ΚΑΙ ΦΙΛΩΝΟΣ ΙΟΥΔΑΙΩΝ
ΠΡΟΣ ΜΟΝΑΧΟΝ ΤΙΝΑ

THE GREEK TEXT

EDITED WITH INTRODUCTION AND NOTES, TOGETHER WITH A
DISCUSSION OF

CHRISTIAN POLEMICS AGAINST THE JEWS

INAUGURAL DISSERTATION FOR THE DEGREE OF DOCTOR OF
PHILOSOPHY IN THE UNIVERSITY OF MARBURG

PRESENTED BY

ARTHUR CUSHMAN McGIFFERT

NEW YORK
THE CHRISTIAN LITERATURE COMPANY
1889

PREFACE.

In the fall of 1887, while engaged in collating manuscripts in the National Library at Paris, I found an entry in the catalogue which at once aroused my curiosity. Codex Græc. 1111 was said to contain, among other works, *Papisci et Jasonis Judæorum cum monacho quodam de christiana religione et Mosaïca lege colloquium.* Upon examining the manuscript, I discovered that the title was incorrect (the name *Jasonis* being substituted for *Philonis*), and that the work mentioned, although itself in the form of a dialogue, unfortunately had no connection with the lost second-century Dialogue of Papiscus and Jason. It proved, however, to possess considerable intrinsic merit, and to be an excellent example of Christian polemics against the Jews; and, being particularly interested in the latter subject, I took the pains to transcribe the whole dialogue.

Afterward my attention was called by Professor Harnack to a note in his *Texte und Untersuchungen*, Bd. I., Heft 3, p. 126, which contained the information that Professor Zahn had discovered, in a MS. in St. Mark's Library, at Venice, a dialogue with a title similar to the one found by myself. He had concluded that there was no relationship between it and the lost Dialogue of Papiscus and Jason, and had not transcribed it. Upon examination it proved to be an older and shorter recension of the Paris dialogue, and is therefore laid at the base of the text given in the following pages.

Still later I learned from a communication made to Professor Harnack by Dr. Oscar von Gebhardt, that the same dialogue is extant in a third MS. in the library of the Most Holy Synod at Moscow. This MS. I have not seen, but my thanks are due to the librarian, who kindly furnished me with its variant readings for a part of the dialogue.

Shortly before completing my work, I discovered that a large part of the material of the dialogue is incorporated in a series of tracts (published by Mai), bearing the common title *Adversus Judæos Disputatio*, and ascribed to Anastasius (see p. 17). The discovery caused me to doubt, for a time, the advisability of publishing the text of the dialogue; but further examination of the work of Anastasius revealed such extensive and important differences between the two writings, that I was confirmed in my original intention. Anastasius' tracts throw new light upon the composition of the dialogue, and the relationship between the two furnishes an interesting chapter in the history of Christian literature. The interest which the latter possessed for me was due in a great part to its representative character as one of a large and important class of works which historians have greatly neglected. A thorough discussion of that class of writings is not attempted in this brief dissertation, but the effort has been made to give, in the first chapter of the Introduction, something of an idea of its nature and extent.

The substance of the first and last paragraphs of the Introduction appeared as a separate article, under the title, "Christian Polemics against the Jews," in the *Presbyterian Review* for July, 1888.

ARTHUR CUSHMAN McGIFFERT.

CONTENTS.

	PAGE
PREFACE	iii
INTRODUCTION	1
CHAPTER I.—CHRISTIAN POLEMICS AGAINST THE JEWS.	1
§ 1. The Nature of the Polemics	1
§ 2. List of Anti-Jewish Works	12
CHAPTER II.—DIALOGUE OF PAPISCUS AND PHILO	28
§ 3. Manuscripts	28
§ 4. Relation between the two forms of the Dialogue	31
§ 5. Relation of the Dialogue to other Anti-Jewish Works	32
§ 6. Sources and Title	37
§ 7. Time and Place of Composition. Authorship	41
§ 8. Analysis of the Dialogue	44
THE TEXT	49
NOTES	85
SCRIPTURE REFERENCES	93

INTRODUCTION.

CHAPTER I.

CHRISTIAN POLEMICS AGAINST THE JEWS.

§ 1. *The Nature of the Polemics.*

It lies in the very nature of the case that Christian polemics against the Jews should begin at an early date. The first problem which confronted the church when it began to come to self-consciousness and to reflect upon its own position was to determine its relation to Judaism. Its founder was held to be the Jewish Messiah, and yet he was rejected with scorn by the Jewish nation. His followers claimed for him all the rights and honors of that Messiah, but those rights and honors were denied him by his own people. There remained but one possibility open: the Jewish people were mistaken. The first problem of the Christian church was to prove this. All the circumstances of the age emphasized this need. Religion was at that time practically a national institution. Each nation had its own religion, and was left by the Roman power in undisturbed possession of it so long as it remained within its national limits. But Christianity, Jewish in its origin, was repudiated by the nation in whose bosom it had been born, and thus, as a religion severed from national life, it contradicted all the principles of the age. Again, the worth of a religion then was measured to a great extent by its antiquity. But Christianity, if the standpoint of the Jews were admitted, was nothing better than a novel superstition—without national approval, without the honor of antiquity. In this dilemma, felt very early by the church and felt with ever increasing force, there remained but the one course: to show to the world, first, that Christianity was the true Judaism, the true national faith, and secondly, that the Judaism of the day was in consequence a perversion of it and a departure from it. To prove the former it was necessary to show that Christ was the promised Messiah, whom the Jews themselves admitted would found a new order of things when he should come, to show that Christianity was the higher Judaism of the Messianic kingdom. There was but one way to proceed in the demonstration; the Jews' accepted book must be shown to prophesy of Christ and of his church. The search for Messianic prophecies began then at the very start. We see the results of it in the New Testament itself. Had the life of Christ corresponded so exactly with the expectations of the age, with the prevalent idea of the Messiah, that no doubt could exist in any one's mind that he was the promised Messiah, the effort to prove him such would of course have been superfluous. But this was not the case. The life of Christ contained so many elements apparently quite at variance with the Messianic prophecies that the disciples felt at the very start the need of justifying their belief in him, and that to themselves as well as to the Jews. They would have felt the need had there been no hostile Jews to impress it upon them. They might have accepted Christ as the founder of a new religion entirely independent of and severed from all connection with Judaism, as Marcion did; but this could never have occurred to them as Jews trained in the expectation of a Messiah. A deliverer was to come —the Messiah. Christ came to deliver; he could be to his disciples no one else than the Messiah, however much his life seemed to contradict the accepted Messianic ideas. The only alternative left them was to find themselves mistaken in their earlier interpretation of the Old Testament, and to find in it, with the key of Christ's actual life, predictions corresponding with that life.

But if the disciples were right in their views of Christ, the Jews must be wrong, and thus was felt the pressure to prove directly the falsity of their position, to prove, that is, that non-Christian Judaism was a perversion of true, divinely ordained Judaism. This second stage appears early. The Epistle of Barnabas is its classic monument. The necessity which lay upon the early church was a matter which concerned its very existence, and that entirely independent of all personal connection with the Jews, independent of any purpose of propagandism among them. Had no Jew attacked the claims of Christ as the Messiah, there would still have lain upon the church the necessity of self-justification. The substance of anti-Jewish polemics would have remained; it would simply have lost its polemic tone. This fact explains a remarkable feature of the polemics which characterizes it throughout. It shows itself, in fact, almost entirely regardless of the Jews themselves, and though cast in the form of polemics against them, seems to be aimed far less at them than at an entirely different public. The persuasion of the Jews, their refutation for the purpose of winning them, seems to be the last consideration with the author. Of all the anti-Jewish dialogues of which we know, but three (the dialogue of Simon and Theophilus being counted as a reproduction of that of Papiscus and Jason) result in the conversion of the Jew. In the remainder, whether the Jew plays his rôle throughout, as in Justin's dialogue with Trypho, or whether he drops entirely from the scene before the completion of the work, as in our present dialogue, he is at best but a lay figure, a sort of artistic setting. The artificial character runs in fact through all these dialogues. The real opponent of the Christian is not the Jew but the unbeliever in general, as the Christian imagines him, that is, his apology is directed not toward the Jewish nation merely, but toward the whole non-Christian world. This characteristic emphasizes itself more and more as time advances. From the speech of Peter on the day of Pentecost, when the Jews were addressed and the apology for Christianity was directed to them alone, to the dialogues and treatises of subsequent centuries is a great step. As the Jewish nation would not accept Christianity, Christianity must break with it, and that it did right early. And as it extended itself in the heathen world the Jews became a factor of ever decreasing importance. The artificial character of which we have spoken is excellently illustrated by a passage in our dialogue which states the author's purpose in composing it—or rather that of the latest editor in revising it : " We have quoted these few things from many contained in the Holy Prophets *for the sake of confirming the faith of us Christians*, and as a rebuke to the Jews' pride and hardness of heart." With this passage are to be compared the words of Isidore, in the introduction to his work *Contra Judæos*, in which, while the refutation of the Jews is to be sure mentioned, it is looked upon as a matter of secondary importance. But in these two passages it is not the defense of Christianity over against the heathen world that is emphasized, but rather the confirmation of the faith of the believers themselves. In that age it could not, of course, be otherwise. That which had begun in the time of the first disciples as actual polemics was continued as a confirmation for believers after the urgent necessity for polemics had ceased. This is but the history of Christian apologetics in general. Arguments which have been forged in the heat of battle to be used as weapons against assailants are one by one beaten into plowshares for the cultivation of the conquered territory. The fact which has been emphasized assists us in estimating properly the historical importance of the whole class of works with which we are concerned. Is the Jew but a lay figure, we realize at once that we can learn little from these works as to the actual relations between Jews and Christians. Polemics which would be continued, even if the personal object of attack vanished, will mirror very imperfectly the real position of that antagonist. In fact, if we wish to learn the actual attitude of the Jews toward Christianity we must seek elsewhere than in the Christian works which have been directed against them. This fact, which lies in the nature of the case, is well illustrated by the actual procedure of the Jewish figure in all of our dialogues. For the most part, his rôle is simply to assist the Christian in his demonstration by suggesting just such points, and asking just such questions, as furnish the needed steps in the discussion of the latter. He rarely impedes the demonstration in the slightest degree. This irrelevancy is particularly noticeable in the opening paragraph of our dialogue, in which the Jew is made to object to the Christian's worship of images, as if it could be of any possible consequence to the Christian church of that age, what the Jews might think of their practice. This section, of course, is intended as a defense of the practice over against the attacks of iconoclastic Christians, with whom the strife was then raging. The historical value of this class of works is greatly diminished by this general consideration. We can seek at most only for occasional notices of the contemporary external condition of the Jews, such as the references in the present work to the Christian occupation of the Jews' sacred places, etc.[1] Of the real attitude of the Jews toward the Christians, of the nature of their polemics against Christianity, if they still troubled themselves with such polemics, these works tell us nothing.

During the early years of Christianity the Old Testament was the only book of oracles for Christians as well as for Jews. To it and it alone could they appeal for a written warrant for their teaching. They must find in it then, not simply prophecies of the

[1] The work of Thaddæus Pelusiota (see next paragraph) furnishes a few curious and interesting historic details; of which at some future time.

external life of the individual Jesus, but also the whole plan of salvation as understood by them. It must, in fact, be their Gospel,¹ and what Christ and his apostles taught must be found taught there too. The part which the Old Testament played in the early church was thus prodigious. Had Christ come with a written Gospel in his hand, as Mohammed came with the Koran, all would have been different. As it was, Jews and Christians had but one book, in which the Jews read one thing, the Christians quite another. But as in course of time Christianity came into possession of its own independent book, as the writings of the disciples began to circulate and to be looked upon as possessing divine authority, the state of affairs was changed. The church was no longer confined to the Old Testament. And yet, though the church had by this time broken completely its Jewish bonds and had become universal in spirit and in principle, though it was composed largely of Gentiles, to whom Judaism was far from sacred, still the Old Testament had during the earlier years gained, under the necessities of the case, so completely the stamp of a Christian book, and under Christian interpretation had lost so completely its Jewish character, that it was preserved as a most necessary part of the Scripture canon of the church. It is to the necessity laid upon the early church to make of it a Christian book, that we owe its existence to-day in the canon. Later centuries, with their apostolic works and with their independence over against Judaism, would never have felt the need of so transforming it. But the process thus begun under necessity was most naturally continued after the necessity was past. Once given the Old Testament as a Christian book no generation of the church could be foolish enough to throw aside such a treasure. Once established the practice of reading it in a spiritual sense, its inexhaustibleness assured its permanent use.

Christian apologetics is of three kinds: that which appeals to prophecy, that which appeals to reason, and that which appeals to history—not to imply, of course, that these three kinds are always kept distinct in practice. The original relation of Christianity to Judaism necessarily gave to the earliest Christian apologetics the form of an appeal to prophecy. But as the church began to face more and more the heathen world, which had neither the opportunity nor the inclination to examine the Jewish Scriptures and to test the proofs of the Christians drawn from this source, as in fact

¹ Cf. Harnack, *Texte und Untersuchungen*, Vol. I. Heft 3, p. 57.

it faced a world with whom this common ground was wanting, it had recourse necessarily to the second form of apologetics. Christianity must be shown to be rational, not simply ordained by the God of the Jewish Scriptures. This second form begins with the works of the Greek apologists of the second century. But even here it was not only external pressure, but also internal intellectual need, which gave rise to this kind of thinking and writing. Christians sought confirmation in their faith, justification for their belief. Jewish Christians had sought it in the sanction of the national God, whose word, recorded in their national Scriptures, was law to them. Greek Christians, trained in the atmosphere of philosophy, sought it in the sanction of their reason. But the second kind of apologetics by no means drove out the first. The use of the Hebrew prophets for the confirmation of the Christian faith was not confined to Jewish Christians. Begun by them, it was taken up and pursued eagerly by the heathen converts. But to them the Old Testament played a different rôle. To Jewish Christians it was in and of itself the word of God. Its prophecies had a worth, therefore, independent of the life of Christ. To heathen Christians it was the word of God *only* because it prophesied of Christ. To the latter, therefore, it was at first valuable only in so far as it contained predictions and types of the Messiah and his church. By them was felt, therefore, far more keenly than by Jewish Christians, the need of finding for every part of the Old Testament a correspondence in the life of Christ, and it is to them, more than to Jewish Christians, that we owe its transformation from a historical book to a thesaurus of divine oracles. Jewish Christians would have remained satisfied to find in the historical books national history, in the prophetical books, to a certain extent, national prophecies. It was not necessary for the life of Christ to exhaust the whole mass of Old Testament predictions. But to the heathen the Old Testament as a national book could have no meaning. It must not only include Christianity, it must be wholly Christian.

An argument from prophecy has always had great weight with the human mind. There enters into it so prominent an element of supernaturalness as to give it a peculiar force. The gentile Christian church found itself in possession of books written centuries before the advent of their Christ, which, as the Jewish Christians had already pointed out to them, foretold a Messiah and a Messianic kingdom identical with their Messiah and his kingdom. They did not need to ask as to the divinity of these books; they did not need to accept them first as Jewish Scriptures. They accepted them at once as divine and as Christian books because they prophesied of Christ. To them they were at first that and nothing more. Before them then lay the task, undertaken with a very different motive from that of the Jewish Christians, of making the two elements, prophecy and fulfillment, fit not simply in part but completely, of co-ordinating them throughout. With the Jewish Christians it was enough to prove from the Scriptures that Christ was the promised Messiah of the Jews. To the heathen Christians that could of itself have no meaning. To them Christ was not the Jewish Messiah but the Saviour of the world and would have remained such had there been no Old Testament. They gladly adopted the latter because, spiritualized as they spiritualized it, it proved to them the antiquity of their religion and furnished them in its prophecies, so wonderfully fulfilled, welcome testimony to the divine origin of their religion.

These two kinds of apologetics then run alongside one another—each playing an important part in the literary activity of the early church. It is noticeable, however, that they are usually in the earlier centuries kept quite distinct. We have apologies of the first class and apologies of the second class, but not combinations of the two kinds. As an example of the first, for instance, may be cited Justin Martyr's Dialogue with Trypho, of the second, his apologies; so Tertullian's *Adversus Judæos* on the one hand, and his apology on the other. This must of necessity have been the mode of procedure in the earliest generations, when the two classes of assailants, the Jews and the heathen, were so sharply distinct. To represent to the Jews the rationality of Christianity was useless. To them only the Scriptures had weight. To appeal to the heathen from the Scriptures, when they knew nothing of the Old Testament, would have been absurd. In the first generations of Christianity, Judaism played an important rôle in the ranks of its antagonists. In spite, therefore, of what has been said as to the necessary inward impulse toward apologetics, it is certain that at first there was felt very forcibly the external need also. The Jews were a real and formidable enemy then, and they were besides a people among whom the church hoped to propagate Christianity. The continued independent use of the first class of apologetics, even after the second had begun, is therefore not to be wondered at. It is further quite natural that this class of apologetics should continue to bear he name *Adversus Judæos* long after the Jews had ceased to play a part of any consequence among the enemies of the church. The two classes began as *Adv. Judæos* and *Adv. Nationes*, the one biblical, the other rational. It was most natural that all works in which Old Testament prophecies were exhibited as proofs of the truth of Christianity should continue to be thrown into that form, even after they had ceased to be directed against the Jews themselves. In order to give force and vividness—still more in order to give, so to speak, an excuse for a composition of this kind, there must be supposed an opponent contradicting the truth of the Christian's conclusions, and who else could this be than the Jew? And this must have been true also of works not cast in the form of a dialogue. Wherever Old Testament prophecies are appealed to, there the Jew is naturally thought of as the one who disputes the Christian's conclusions. To justify any apology there must be an opponent real or imagined. If there is no actual one, and the work is written simply to confirm the faith of believers, then an opponent must be imagined to exist—in the present case of course a Jew. We know that before many centuries had passed the Jews had dropped entirely out of consideration among the Christians in most parts of the empire, that the church no longer feared them and no longer came into actual conflict with them. And yet the nominal apologies addressed to the Jews continue even down to the end of the middle ages, their artificial character of course strongly marked.

Another point must be noticed in connection with this class of apologetics. Prophecy is the correlate of history. What prophecy foretells, history fulfills. A work devoted, therefore, to the demonstration of the truth of Christianity upon the basis of prophecy must confine itself to the realm of history. Dogmatics can properly play no part in such a work, for it is absurd to speak of a dogma as being prophesied, when the dogma is itself ostensibly drawn from the very book which prophesies. If the dogma embodies the assertion of a fact which has occurred or is supposed to have occurred in history, the predictions which may be cited in proof of its truth are cited of course for the fact as such, not for the dogma about the fact. And such dogmas as have to do with eternal truths can of course have no relation to prophecy. Dogmas vary from age to age. But in apologetics based upon prophecy we have two unchangeable factors: Old Testament predictions, New Testament fulfillment. In the generations before the formation of the New Testament canon the second factor was, to be sure, variable. The traditions as to the life of Christ were not yet absolutely fixed, and opportunity was given to alter and add to them at will, a process of which we can detect many traces in the writings of the second century. But after the New Testament canon was established this process ceased. The factors were fixed, and there remained only the discovery on the part of sharp-sighted and keen-witted men of new coincidences between the two. The framework within which all such search must proceed was unalterably settled. This is the natural cause of the stereotyped character of this class of apologetics, which is very marked throughout. It is not surprising that in a work of the middle ages devoted to prophecy and its fulfillment we should find the same general matter as in a work of the earliest centuries. It could not be otherwise. The contents of the life of Christ had long been fixed, and with that prophecy had chiefly to do. (The fulfillment of prophecy in the later history of the church is for the present left out of consideration.) The ordinary marks of the doctrinal views of the author, from which we are accustomed to judge as to the age of his work, we have no right to expect. If they occur, they are misnomers and inconsistencies in the work. At the same time they do occur, illogically, very frequently.[1] In fact, the works in which an indication of date cannot be gathered from their doctrinal tone are largely in the minority. But in spite of this the natural character of these works is archaic. The theological passages do not form their chief characteristic.

We have spoken of two classes of apologetics. To these is to be added the third, already enumerated: apologetics based upon history; that is, apologetics in which the history of the church and of its enemies is appealed to as a proof of its divine origin. This class is, of course, of later growth. Only when Christianity had a history behind it, could it make use of that history as an argument. Strictly speaking, this is of course an appeal to reason. The preservation of the church in the midst of persecution, its continued prosperity, its benefits to the human race—these were so many

---

[1] Much oftener than one might gather from Harnack's remarks. Besides the Pseudo-Gregorian *Testimonia* which he mentions, the dialogue of Gregentius with Herbano the Jew is permeated with the theological atmosphere of the sixth century. and the same general fact is true of many later works, especially of the scholastics.

appeals to the reason of man for the divine origin of Christianity. But in the present instance the history of the church served a double purpose in the realm of apologetics. Not only did it furnish of itself a direct argument, but in fulfilling Scripture predictions it increased the sum of proofs from prophecy. The Old Testament was found to contain not only prophecies of Christ, but also of his church, and indeed of subsequent world history in large proportions. In this way the argument from history by itself, and the argument from prophecy fulfilled in it became closely joined and were continually used together. This was more and more the case as time advanced. The numerical predictions of Daniel play a rôle of constantly increasing prominence. And at the same time, partly in connection with these predictions and partly independent of them, the contrasts were drawn with ever more minuteness of detail between the prosperity of the Christians and the ill-fortune of their Jewish adversaries. The dark lot of the latter formed an excellent background against which to display the brilliant history of the former. Works in which this style of argument is prominent gain a degree of vividness and life-likeness, which makes it seem that they must be directed against real Jewish opponents and be sprung from the actual heat of conflict, and yet we are not safe in drawing this conclusion upon this ground alone. But these historical sections will at the same time usually be found to give us welcome data for fixing the age of the works in which they occur. The subject can scarcely be developed without contemporaneous events leaving their impress, and at this point we must look for most light as to the composition of the various works, and also for the most matter of interest, because matter least stereotyped.

The literary form of the works *Adversus Judæos* is threefold. We have dialogues between Christians and Jews; we have regular treatises in the form of apologies, or of attacks, or of both ; and we have *Testimonia*, which are but a massing together of Old Testament predictions, arranged according to the events which they foretell. The first is a favorite form. A glance at the list given in § 2 will show that quite a proportion of all anti-Jewish works are dialogues. It was a form suggested by the very nature of the material. In no way could the force of the Old Testament predictions be better brought out than by supposing their proper interpretation disputed by the Jew, who is then obliged to yield his view to that of the Christian. The nature of the subject necessitated a constant change from one topic to another which was peculiarly fitted to dialogistic discourse.[1] For the explanation of the prevalence of this form in anti-Jewish works it is, therefore, unnecessary to assume the influence of the dialogues of Justin and Trypho, or of Papiscus and Jason. It is plain, of course, that we cannot conclude the actual existence of the parties named in the dialogue. They may be, as they probably most often are, fictitious characters.

The second form mentioned treats the subject in essentially the same manner as the first. The formal introduction of the two contending parties is merely an externality which hardly affects the disposition of the material. Many of the regular treatises could be transformed into dialogues by the mere insertion of names. The similarity between the two classes is so great that the one form may pass quite easily into the other, even within the same work; as, for instance, in the work we are to consider, in which the form of the dialogue disappears entirely long before its conclusion.

The third form mentioned is quite different from the other two. Its representatives are the *Testimonia* of Cyprian and of Pseudo-Gregory. It is an illustration of what has been said of the natural tendency to throw all works which deal with prophecy into the form of anti-Jewish polemics, that even these *Testimonia*, which in form are the farthest possible from polemical works, still bear the title *Adv. Judæos*. But it must be remarked that the distinguishing characteristic of all the three classes which we have been considering is not the fact that they are formally directed against the Jews—this, though so universal, is but an accident, not an essential property upon which the classification depends. The essential characteristic is the use of Old Testament prophecies. And thus, though the lost *Eclogæ* of Melito, for instance, were not, so far as we know, brought formally into any connection with the Jews, they nevertheless belong to the general class of works under consideration, just as much as the *Testimonia* of Cyprian and of Pseudo-Gregory, whose titles expressly name the Jews. They will therefore be included in our list of anti-Jewish works. At the same time there are, on the other hand, works against the Jews which are purely polemical, being devoted solely to an exhibition of the wickedness of the Jews, and containing no element of apology for Christianity, no attempt to prove its

[1] *Cf.* the preface to the *Dialogus Gualteri et Balduini* (Migne, ccix. 426), and the passage quoted from Richard's work *De Emmanuele libri duo* (*infra* p. 26).

truth in any respect. Such writings have no connection with the class of works under consideration, although the word "Jews" appears in their titles. They will, therefore, be omitted in our list.[1]

§ 2. List of Anti-Jewish Works.

The following list is designed to contain all ancient and mediæval Greek and Latin works of the class under consideration with whose titles the writer is acquainted, whether extant or non-extant. He has endeavored to make it as exhaustive as possible, but by no means pretends to claim for it absolute completeness, for he is well aware that some works may have escaped his notice. The list is, of course, not intended to include writings upon other subjects which deal with the Jews only indirectly or in passing. Such works are legion. Anti-Jewish polemics are scattered through innumerable dogmatic treatises, homilies, and especially commentaries. For Latin works the writer has been aided in his search by the subject index of Migne's *Patrologia Latina*. For the Greek Patrology unfortunately no such index as yet exists.[2]

I. Greek works.

1. *Dialogue of Papiscus and Jason.*

This dialogue is no longer extant, but we can obtain an excellent idea of its general character from the Dialogue of Simon and Theophilus which Harnack (*Texte und Untersuchungen*, Bd. I., Heft 3, pp. 1-36) has proved almost beyond the shadow of a doubt to be a free reproduction of it. For a summary of what we know in regard to the original work see *ibid.* p. 116 ff., and for a comparison of it with our dialogue see § 5 below.

2. Justin Martyr : *Dialogue with Trypho.*
3. Melito : *Eclogæ.*

This work, which is no longer extant, was not directed against the Jews, but it may be mentioned in this connection because it

---

[1] The writer has in mind particularly certain works by Agobard : *de insolentia Judæorum* (Migne, civ. 69-76), *de baptismo Judæorum* (*ib.* 101-106), *de cavendo convictu et Societate Judaica* (107-114). The epistle *Severi Episcopi Majoricensis de Judæis* (Migne, xx. 731-746) has nothing to do either with polemics or apologetics, but is simply an account of the conversion of a multitude of Jews in the island of Majorca.

[2] The list given in Fabricius-Harles, VI. 748 ff. is very incomplete, but has been of especial use in directing the writer's attention to works as yet unpublished.

contained "extracts from the law and the prophets concerning the Saviour and our entire faith," and thus seems to have been a work of the same nature as the *Testimonia* of Cyprian and Pseudo-Gregory. The following passage from a fragment of a work of "Meliton the Bishop *On Faith*" (given by Cureton, *Spic. Syriac*, p. 52 ff.), whether it has reference to the *Eclogæ* or not, at least points to a work of the same kind, and to one which was highly developed in the details of Christ's life : "We have made collections from the Law and the Prophets relative to those things which have been declared respecting our Lord Jesus Christ, that we may prove to your love that he is perfect Reason, the Word of God ; who was begotten before the light ; who was creator together with the Father ; who was the fashioner of man; who was all in all ; who among the patriarchs was patriarch ; who in the law was law ; among priests chief priest ; amongst kings governor ; among prophets the prophet ; among the angels archangel ; in the Voice the word ; among spirits spirit ; in the Father the Son ; in God, God the King forever and ever; who was with Noah, Abram . . . (etc.) ; who in David and the prophets foretold his own sufferings ; who was incarnate in the Virgin ; who was born in Bethlehem ; who was wrapped in swaddling clothes in the manger ; who was seen of the shepherds ; who was glorified of the angels ; who was worshiped of the Magi ; who was pointed out by John ; who assembled the apostles; who preached the kingdom ; who healed the maimed ; who gave light to the blind ; who raised the dead ; who appeared in the temple ; who was not believed in by the people ; who was betrayed by Judas ; who was laid hold on by the priests ; who was condemned by Pilate ; who was transfixed in the flesh ; who was hanged upon the tree ; who was buried in the earth ; who rose from the dead ; who appeared to the apostles ; who ascended into heaven ; who sitteth on the right hand of the Father; who is the rest of those that have departed, the recoverer of those that were lost, the light of those who were in darkness, the deliverer of those who are captives, the guide of those who have gone astray, the refuge of the afflicted, the bridegroom of the church, the charioteer of the cherubim, the captain of the angels, God who is of God, the Son who is of the Father, Jesus Christ the King forever and ever. Amen." Otto and others hold that this fragment is actually from a work of Melito, but Harnack (*Texte und Untersuchungen*, Vol. I., Heft 1, p. 268) considers it an extract from a work of Irenæus.

4. Miltiades: *Adversus Judæos.*
Of this work, which is no longer extant, we know only through Eusebius, who mentions it in *H. E.* v. 17. 5, and informs us that it existed in two volumes.[1]

5. *Fragmentum incogniti operis adversus Judæos.*
Under this title Mai (*Script. vet. nova coll.* viii. 2. 26) gives a brief fragment in Greek which bears the name of Sylvester, and is printed in Migne (*Patr. Lat.* viii. 814) among the works of Pope Sylvester. The fragment is too brief to permit much of a judgment as to the character of the work, or even to make it certain that it is from a work against the Jews. It is devoted to an illustration of the two natures in Christ.

6. Hippolytus: *Demonstratio adversus Judæos.*
Only a fragment exists (Migne, *Patr. Græc.* x. 787–794), which is devoted chiefly to the passion of Christ and to the agency of the Jews in it, with prophecies foretelling it and the consequent punishment of the Jews. One passage is quite similar to a passage in our dialogue (see p. 90), but no literary relationship between the two works can be constituted from the fragment which we have. According to Bunsen (*Hippolytus and his Age,* Vol. I., p. 265) "The anonymous author of the 'Acta Martyrum,' gives in Appendix III. (pp. 449–488), the text of an old Latin translation of a considerable part of the fragment preserved to us in Greek. He had discovered it among the spurious works ascribed to Cyprian. The title is 'Demonstratio adversus Judæos.' It begins exactly with the first words of our Greek fragment, which cannot have been the opening of the address, but was probably the beginning of the peroration. The Greek text forms the first two chapters of this very remarkable fragment. What follows (ch. 3–7, pp. 452b–458) is far more interesting than the part preserved in the Greek text. The author no longer appeals to sacred texts of their prophets; he speaks to their hearts, he appeals to the spirit in them. 'The eye of the mind,' he says, 'is the spirit; through him things spiritual are seen; if therefore you are spiritual, you understand

---

[1] Eusebius (*H. E.* IV. 27) mentions among the writings of Apolinarius of Hierapolis a work πρὸς Ἰουδαίους πρῶτον καὶ δεύτερον. The words however are wanting in many manuscripts and also in Rufinus and in Jerome, and are therefore to be regarded as a later insertion. Fabricius mentions the work in his list, but with the notice of Eusebius shown to be spurious no trace of the existence of such a writing remains.

heavenly things. For like knows (understands) what is like to it.' These words may be considered as the theme of the whole. Hence we see that we have not an attack upon the Jews in this treatise, but an address to them, an appeal to their conscience and intellect. The character of the treatise is that of an eloquent writer, who had studied Plato, and who had not only a deep Christian intellect, but also a heart full of Christ, and of love to his brethren." Harnack (*Op. cit.* p. 75) refers to Bunsen's notice, but says that he knows nothing about the Latin fragment mentioned. I have not myself seen it, and know only what Bunsen states.

7. Diodorus Tarsensis : *Contra Judæos.*

This work, which is no longer extant, is mentioned in the list given by Fabricius-Harles, Vol. VI., p. 747. Suidas (who is there referred to) gives a list of the writings of Diodorus (art. *Diodorus*), upon the authority of Θεόδωρος Ἀναγνώστης ἐν τῇ Ἐκκλησιαστικῇ Ἱστορίᾳ. The list includes the *Contra Judæos.*

8. Hieronymus Græcus: *Dialogus Christiani cum Judæo de Trinitate.*

In Migne, xl. 847–859. A dialogue of an entirely theological character, as indicated by the title. The Old Testament is used only as a source of proof texts for the doctrine of the Trinity, and not as a book of prophecies.

9. *Testimonia adversus Judæos.*

Although this work was ascribed to Gregory of Nyssa and printed by Migne (xlvi. 193–234) among his writings, it was composed long after his time. It is of the same general nature as the *Testimonia* of Cyprian, giving detailed prophecies of the life of Christ, but in its first paragraph is quite theological, containing the fully developed doctrine of the Trinity. For further details in regard to this work and its relation to our dialogue, see § 5 below.

10. Chrysostom: *Adversus Judæos et Gentiles demonstratio quod Christus sit Deus.*

In Migne's *Patr. Græc.* xlviii. 813–838. The first part of this work is composed chiefly of Old Testament prophecies, foretelling that the Christ to come was to be a God, and predicting the manner and place of his advent, the commission of the apostles, the casting out of the Jews, the last judgment, etc. The latter part is devoted to a brief account of the prosperity of the church and of the attacks of various emperors upon the Christians.

11. Chrysostom : *Adversus Judæos Orationes,* viii.

In Migne, *ib.* 843-892. Eight long orations devoted rather to positive attacks upon the Jews than to the defense of Christianity. The predictions in regard to the life of Christ play but a small part, while those in regard to the conduct and condition of the Jews are dwelt upon at great length.

12. Cyril of Alexandria : *Libri de Synagoge defectu.*

This work is no longer extant, but Migne (*Patr. Græc.* lxxvi. 1421-1424) gives a brief fragment upon the change of the name Abram to Abraham, which perhaps formed a part of the lost work.

13. Basil of Seleucia : *Contra Judæos de Salvatoris adventu demonstratio* (*Oratio* xxxviii.).

In Migne, *ib.* lxxxv. 400-425. This work is devoted chiefly to a numerical calculation as to the time of the Messiah's advent and the destruction of Jerusalem, resulting in the proof that Jesus is the Messiah. As a consequence the prophecies of Daniel play a large part in the work.

14. Philip of Side : *Acta Disputationis de Christo in Perside inter Christianos, Gentiles ac Judæos habitæ.*

This work, or a fragment of it, exists in a manuscript in the Imperial Library at Vienna. Through the kindness of a friend I have been furnished with the following notice taken from the catalogue of the library : "Philippi, ab urbe Pamphiliæ Sidâ, ubi natus fuit, cognominati Sidetæ, qui sæculo post Christum quarto S. Joannis Chrisostomi fuit presbyter et syncellus, acta disputationis de Christo in Perside inter Christianos, Gentiles ac Judæos habitæ cui ipse interfuit ; excerpta ex amplissimo ipsius opere Historiæ Christianæ in triginta sex libros diviso, et quidem ex eo jam memoratæ Historiæ libro, quo egit de nativitate Christi et de Magis." I am informed that the *Acta Disputationis* fill only the first two leaves of the manuscript.

15. Gregentius of Taphar : *Disputatio cum Herbano Judæo.*

In Migne, lxxxvi. 681-784. A very elaborate account of a dialogue which took place between the Archbishop Gregentius and the Jew Herbanus, in the presence of a vast concourse of Jews and Christians, the king, the senate, etc. The dialogue continues for four days and ends with the conversion and baptism of Herbanus and 5,000,000 other Jews, comprising all the Jews in the kingdom. The conversion is not accomplished however by the arguments of the archbishop, but by the miraculous appearance of Christ himself upon the clouds. The work displays a highly developed theology and christology, and abounds in abstruse discussions upon doctrinal points. At the same time the argument for the Messiahship of Jesus and for the truth of Christianity drawn from prophecy plays a prominent part and appears in quite a developed form. The work closes with an account of the death of Gregentius, and therefore does not pretend to be his own composition. It is certainly later than his time.

16. *Διάλεξις κατὰ Ἰουδαίων*.

Bandini in his *Catalogus Bibl. Mediceæ Laurentianæ*, tom. I., p. 165, has given a brief portion of this work, which is too short to enable much of a judgment to be formed in regard to it. It is not in the form of a dialogue, however, as Harnack says (*Op. cit.* p. 75). The purpose of the work is stated in the first sentence to be to prove to the Jew from the Old Testament that the Saviour Christ was prophesied of old and taught to be divine. It thus ranks itself with the general class of works under consideration.

17. *Dialogue of Timothy and Aquila.*

See Mai, *Spic. Rom.* ix. p. xii. sq., and *Nova Bibl.* vi. ii. p. 537 sq. Mai gives only the beginning and end of this dialogue, from a codex of the Patmos library, but it is enough to prove that it is much later than the time of Cyril, when it pretends to have been written. Many theological expressions betray a later date. The Jew is converted and receives baptism after the dialogue is concluded.

18. Stephen of Bostra : *Contra Judæos.*

This work is no longer extant. We know of it only through John of Damascus, who in his *Third Oration on Images* (Migne, *Patr. Gr.* xciv. 1376) gives two brief quotations from it on the subject of image worship. We know nothing as to the nature of the work as a whole.

19. Anastasius Abbas : *Adversus Judæos Disputatio.*

The Greek original of this work was first published by Mai (*Script. Vet. nova collect.* vii. 207–244) and is contained in Migne's *Patr. Gr.*, lxxxix. 1203–1282. A Latin translation, less full than the Greek, had already been made by Turrianus and published by Canisius in his *Antiq. lect.*, tom. II., part iii., p. 12, ed. Basnagii (according to Mai, *ib.* p. 207 note). The close of the work is wanting. For a detailed description of the work and a comparison of it with our dialogue, see § 5 below.

20. Leontius of Neapolis in Cyprus : *Sermo contra Judæos.*

In Migne, xciii. 1597-1609. The work is devoted exclusively to the subject of image worship. It is throughout an argument *ad hominem*. It is first maintained against the Jews that God commanded Moses to make the cherubim, etc., and then it is declared that the Christians do not worship the wood of the cross itself, but, through it and images of all kinds, God and Christ. Instances are drawn from the Old Testament of the same kind of worship, and the instance of Jacob and Joseph (given also in our dialogue § 1) is cited, but with a slight variation in form (see the notes, p. 85). This line of argument is the same as that pursued by the Christian in our dialogue. The work bears the form of a discourse, but occasionally a Jew and a Christian are introduced as speaking without any apparent reasons.

21. Leontius of Cyprus : *Contra Judæos*.

In Migne, *ib.*, 1609-1612. A fragment, extant only in Latin, of a lost work ascribed to the same author. There is no hint in the fragment itself as to its author.

It contains prophecies from Isaiah, Jeremiah, Micah, etc., which foretell the nature of the Messianic kingdom, its peacefulness and blessedness, and which the author applies to the Christian church.

22. Theodorus Abucara : *Dissertatio cum Judæo (Opuscula* X.).

In Migne, xcvii. 1529-1534. A brief dialogue which is devoted to proving that the Scriptures are to be interpreted of Christ and the Christians, and not literally of the Jews.

23. Euthymius Zigabenus : *Contra Hebræos*.

In Migne, cxxx. 257-305. The first part of the work is devoted chiefly to quotations from the Old Testament in proof of the Trinity, the divinity of Christ, etc., and in prophecy of his birth, crucifixion, resurrection, ascension, the church of the Gentiles, etc. The remainder of the work contains extracts from the orations of Chrysostom against the Jews, from Leontius, John of Damascus and anonymous works.

24. Thaddæus Pelusiota : *Contra Judæos*.

This work has not yet been published. It is extant in three Greek manuscripts in the National Library at Paris (Cod. Græc. 887, 1285, Suppl. Græc. 120) and has been transcribed by the writer with a view to possible publication. It is of considerable extent, perhaps twice as long as the Dialogue of Papiscus and Philo, and dates from the year 1265. The author, Thaddæus Pelusiota, is an otherwise unknown man. The occurrence of the name "Pelusiota" at this late date is very surprising. The work is largely devoted to the miseries of the Jews, all of which are shown to have been prophesied in the Old Testament, and all of which are represented as a punishment for the nation's rejection of Christ. It is urged that the present scattered condition of the Jews is the last captivity foretold in the prophets, a captivity which shall never end because no end has been foretold; and it is maintained that the sin which deserves such an endless captivity for its punishment must have been greater than any that had been committed before the previous captivities. A long passage upon the contrast between the glorious condition of the Christians and the miserable condition of the Jews resembles closely the passage upon the same subject in our present dialogue. The work is very interesting, and in the main far stronger than most anti-Jewish writings. The author was evidently a learned and an able man. His historical references are numerous and many of them curious. The work opens with a passage some pages in length from Josephus' Jewish War, and the works of Eusebius, Chrysostom, Theodoret, Cyril and others are frequently quoted.

25. Andronicus Comnenus: *Dialogus contra Judæos Christiani et Judæi.*

This work has as yet been published only in a Latin version (given by Migne in his *Patr. Gr.*, cxxxiii. 797-924), but the Greek original is extant in a manuscript in the Imperial Library at Vienna (Cod. Græc. 255) according to Lambecius, 2d ed., Vol. V. p. 355 ff. It is in the form of a dialogue, is of great length, and is divided into sixty-four chapters. It is in part very theological, as for instance where it discusses the Trinity, the generation of the Son, the consubstantiality of the Spirit, etc. Other parts are devoted to the prophecies fulfilled in Christ. The Old Testament is used extensively throughout.

26. Georgius of Cyprus: *Contra Marcum ex Jud. Christianum.*

In Migne, cxlii. 247-252. This brief tract is purely theological and has nothing to do with prophecy.

27. Theophanes of Nice: *Contra Judæos libri* vi.

This work has not yet been published. It is extant in three manuscripts in the Paris Library (Cod. Græc. 778, 1249, 1293).

28. John Cantacuzenus: *Adversus Judæos libri novem.*

Likewise unedited and extant in three Paris manuscripts (Cod. Græc. 1243, 1275. Suppl. Græc. 120). It is about twice as long as the work of Thaddæus mentioned above.

29. Nicolaus Hydruntinus: *Dialogus cum Judæo.*
Likewise unedited and extant in Par. Cod. Græc., 1255.
30. Matthæus Hieromonachus: *Libri V. in Judæos.*
Likewise unedited and extant in Par. Cod. Græc., 1293, fol. 119-240, also, according to Fabricius, "in Bodleiana codice Barocc. xxxiii."
31. Gennadius of Constantinople: *Dialogus contra Judæos.*
Likewise unedited and extant in Par. Cod. Græc., 1293, fol. 1-54, and, according to Fabricius, in "MSS. in variis bibliothecis."

II. Latin works.

1. Tertullian: *Adversus Judæos.*
In Oehler's edition of Tertullian's works Vol. II. pp. 701-741. The carnality, particularity and temporality of Judaism over against the spirituality, universality and eternity of Christianity are dwelt upon in the first part of this work. The numerical prophecies of Daniel are then considered at length, and a prominent part is given to a detailed exhibition of the fulfillment of prophecy in the life of Christ. For a comparison of the work with the Dial. of Pap. and Jason see Harnack, *Op. cit.* p. 92 ff. The work makes large use of Justin's *Dial. c. Trypho.* See further § 5, below.

2. Cyprian: *Ad Quirinum (Testimoniorum libri tres).*
In Hartel's *Cypriani opera (Script. eccles. Lat. Vind),* I. 35-184.

These *Testimonia* consist of three books. The first two are composed of collections of Old Testament prophecies foretelling the life of Christ, the Christian church, etc., and thus belong to the general class of works under consideration. The third book is devoted to the graces, virtues, etc., of the Christian life and the sins to be avoided, and is composed chiefly of New Testament passages referring to these subjects. It therefore does not come under consideration in this connection. For a comparison of the work with the Dial. of Pap. and Jason see Harnack (*Op. cit.* p. 97 ff.), and for its relation to our dialogue see § 5, below.

3. Pseudo-Cyprian: *De Montibus Sina et Sion.*
Hartel, iii. 104-119. The spiritual compared with the temporal Israel. Only a limited use is made of prophecy.

4. Pseudo-Cyprian: *Adversus Judæos.*
Ibid. 133-144. In this the idea of the casting out of the Jews and of the acceptance of the Gentiles is emphasized.

5. Celsus : *Ad Vigilium Episcopum de Judaica incredulitate.*
Also printed among the Pseudo-Cyprianic works, *ibid.* 119–132. An arraignment of the Jews for their unbelief in the face of the clear declarations of the prophets in regard to Christ. The Dialogue of Papiscus and Jason is mentioned with high praise, and the author announces that he has himself translated it into Latin. His epistle is really an introduction to the translation which he sends with it to the Bishop Vigilium. The epistle belongs probably to the end of the fifth century (cf. Harnack, *Op. cit.* Bd. I., Heft I., p. 119 ff.).

6. Augustine : *Tractatus adv. Judæos.*
In Migne, *Patr. Lat.* xlii. 51–64. The subject of this tract is in the main the rejection of the literal and the acceptance of the spiritual Israel in their place. It is not in the form of a dialogue, but resembles one somewhat, since the objections of the Jews are quoted and answered one after the other.

7. Pseudo-Augustine : *Contra Judæos Paganos et Arianos Sermo de symbolo.*
In Migne, *ibid.* 1117–1130. The work contains twenty-two chapters, of which four are directed against the Jews. Testimonies for Christ are drawn from the Old and New Testaments, and also from profane writers and from the Sibylline books.

8. Pseudo-Augustine : *De altercatione ecclesiæ et synagogæ Dialogus.*
In Migne, *ibid.* 1131–1140. A dialogue between the church and the synagogue, personified as two women. The general subject is the same as that of the Augustinian *Tractatus* mentioned above. The synagogue confesses herself beaten at every point, and concludes "Ergo omnes ad te venerunt," etc., which indicates the scope of the work.

9. Evagrius : *Altercatio Simonis Judæi et Theophili Christiani.*
See Harnack's *Texte und Untersuchungen*, Bd. I., Heft 3, where this dialogue is shown to be a free reproduction of the lost dialogue of Papiscus and Jason. See also § 5, below.

10. Maximus of Turin : *Tractatus contra Judæos.*
In Migne, lvii. 793–806. This work is, in many respects, similar to the earlier works against the Jews, containing an attack upon the Jews and an argument for the divinity of the Christ. For the latter a mass of Old and New Testament passages are quoted, of which many are found in the *Testimonia* of Cyprian and other earlier works. The tract is comparatively free from dogmatics.

11. Isidore of Seville : *De fide catholica ex Veteri et Novo Testamento contra Judæos ad Florentinam sororem suam.*
In Migne, lxxxiii. 449-538. The work is in two books. The first is devoted to prophecies from the Old Testament which foretell the career of Christ, beginning with his generation from the Father, and closing with his coming to judge the .world. The details are drawn out with great fullness, more than fifty different events being shown to have been prophesied. The whole resembles closely the long paragraph of the Paris MS. of our Dialogue upon the same subject. The resemblance is not such as to involve literary dependence, but it shows the prevalence of this kind of writing, and shows too that there was a large circle of subjects treated by all such writers, and that the texts quoted were in many cases the same. The second book treats in the same manner the relations of the Jews and Gentiles, including the calling of the Gentiles, the rejection of the Jews, etc., twenty-seven particulars being taken up one after the other. The whole work is intensely Biblical, being devoted exclusively to the fulfillment of Old Testament prophecy in Christ and in his church. It is thus one of the very best examples of the kind of works under consideration—apologies based upon prophecy.

12. Agobard : *Epistola de Judaicis superstitionibus.*
In Migne, civ. 77-100. This epistle can hardly be regarded as belonging to the class of works under consideration, since it is chiefly devoted to a mere account of the folly and wickedness of the Jews, and of their enmity against the Christians. A few prophecies are however quoted which are interpreted as foretelling the bad fortunes of Jews and the prosperity of the Christians. In so far therefore the work contains an argument from prophecy, and may thus be mentioned in this connection. Three other epistles by Agobard given by Migne do not come into consideration here. (See note at the close of the preceding paragraph.)

13. Amulo : *Liber contra Judæos.*
In Migne, cxvi. 141-184. This work was originally published under the name of Rabanus, but the authors of the *Hist. lit. Gal.* ascribed it to Amulo (d. 852), and they are followed by Migne. The work, like the preceding, is chiefly devoted to the wickedness and unbelief of the Jews, for which illustrations are drawn from the Fathers and from history. But since some sections of the work contain prophecies from Scripture pointing to Christ as the Messiah, it may claim a place in our list.

14. Fulbertus : *Tractatus contra Judæos.*

In Migne, cxli. 306-318. In this work the Old Testament is freely used to prove the Messiahship of Christ. The prophecy of Gen. xlix. 10, plays an important part in the argument. In one section the details of Christ's life to the number of fourteen are mentioned. The passages in proof of them are however simply referred to, not quoted. This section of course contains many particulars in common with our dialogue and with other earlier works, but betrays no literary connection with them.

15. Petrus Damianus : *Antilogus contra Judæos.*

In Migne, cxlv. 41-57. The work is chiefly devoted to the Scripture proofs of the Trinity, of Christ's Messiahship and Godmanhood, and of the fact that the Messiah has already come in his person. For the Trinity the familiar passages of Genesis, which seem to imply a plurality in the Godhead, are chiefly relied upon.

16. The same : *Dialogus inter Judæum requirentem, et Christianum e contrario respondentem.*

In Migne, *ibid.* 57-68. This work is put in the form of questions and responses. The Jew inquires why, if Christ came not to destroy but to fulfill the law, the Christians do not still observe its precepts. The Christian in reply shows that the law was only mystical and typical, and was fulfilled and therefore done away with by Christ. After completing this subject, the Christian in an epilogue draws out at considerable length the details of Christ's life, quoting Old Testament passages in prophecy of them. Most of the particulars are found in *Papiscus and Philo,* which shows how natural and almost necessary is agreement in connection with this subject, even when literary relationship, as in the present case, cannot be constituted, indeed is quite out of the question.

17. Gilbert : *Tractatus de incarnatione contra Judæos.*

In Migne, clvi. 489-528. This work is divided into three books, of which the first is put in the form of questions embodying objections, and responses containing solutions of them. The first book is devoted chiefly to the conception of the Son of God by the Virgin, and is thoroughly scholastic. The second book, likewise scholastic, discusses *Deus omnia hominis utrum susceperit an non ?* The third book, which alone warrants us in including this work in our list, is devoted particularly to Christ's earthly life as foretold by the prophets, and thus shows many resemblances to our dialogue and other earlier works. Even here however scholasticism plays an important part.

A closing chapter is devoted to Christian image worship, in which the argument deduced in favor of such worship is similar to that in our dialogue, and different from most of the arguments of this age. Not the things themselves, but Christ represented by them, is the object of worship. Many more parallels are drawn from Old Testament history in illustration of this sort of worship than are found in *Papiscus and Philo*. Thurot, in the *Revue Historique*, ii. 105, points out the connection of this work with Gilbert's *History of the Crusades*.

18. Rabbi Samuel Marochianus: *De adventu Messiæ præterito liber*.

In Migne, cxlix. 337-368. This work is peculiar from the fact that it was written by a converted Jew. He demonstrates from the Scriptures, for the benefit of his unconverted countrymen, the truth of Christianity, dwelling at length upon the rejection of the Jews as a result of their treatment of Christ, who is shown from the prophets to be the true Messiah. The tone is very gentle and conciliatory. The work is a translation of an Arabic original.

19. Gilbert, Abbot of Westminster: *Disputatio Judæi cum Christiano de fide christiana*.

Printed among the works of Anselm in Migne, clix. 1005-1036. The author states that the work is a reproduction of an actual disputation between himself and a Jew, and indeed the Jew plays a much more prominent part than is usual in these dialogues, thus giving a character of reality to the discussion. The Jew inquires what authority the Christians have for rejecting the law of Moses. The Christian insists in reply upon the spiritual interpretation of the Old Testament. The prophecy of Gen. xlix. 10 occupies a prominent position in the proof of Christ's Messiahship.

The work contains a lengthy discussion of the continued virginity of Mary and closes with objections against image worship, which the Christian answers by referring to the various images mentioned in the Old Testament (cf. p. 85). A feature of this dialogue is the discussion of the authority of the LXX. which the Jew denies and the Christian maintains. An interesting point is that Baruch iii. 36 is quoted (see p. 88) but denied by the Jew to be the words of Jeremiah, while the Christian contends that they were spoken by Jeremiah and recorded by Baruch.

20. Odo : *Disputatio contra Judæum Leonem nomine de adventu Christi filii Dei.*

In Migne, clx. 1103-1112. A theological disquisition upon the Atonement, thrown into the form of a dialogue between Odo and Leo, and closing with a discussion of Mary's virginity. It makes no use of Scripture prophecies, quoting the Old Testament rarely, and then only in regard to the remission of sins. Only the fact that it assumes the form of a dialogue entitles it to a place in this list.

21. *Dialogus inter Christianum et Judæum de fide catholica.*

Printed in Migne, clxiii. 1015-1072, among the spurious works of Guilelmus Episcopus Calalaunensis. A theological disquisition similar to the preceding, but more scholastic. Old Testament prophecies are used but little, and the work therefore is but slightly connected with the general class of anti-Jewish writings.

22. Rupertus : *Annulus sive Dialogus inter Christianum et Judæum.*

In Migne, clxx. 561-610. The work is in three books, of which the first demonstrates that circumcision no longer avails ; the second discusses chiefly the relation of faith and the Jewish law, and the reason for the rejection of the Jews; and the third is devoted to Scripture proof of Christ's Messiahship. The work therefore falls well into line with the general class of anti-Jewish writings, but at the same time contains much scholasticism. The worship of images is defended by a reference to the images mentioned in the Old Testament, *e. g.*, the brazen serpent, etc. This is a very common argument for the practice, but quite different from that employed in *Papiscus and Philo.* (See p. 85.)

23. Hildebert : *Contra Judæos de incarnatione.* (*Sermones de diversis XIV.*)

Migne, clxxi. 811-814. This brief discourse cites passages from the Old Testament prophetic of the incarnation and of the birth from the Virgin, and shows that the latter is not impossible by referring to many wonders recorded in Scripture, as *e. g.*, the conception of Sarah.

24. Peter, Abbot of Clugny : *Tractatus adversus Judæorum inveteratam duritiem.*

In Migne, clxxxix. 507-650. This lengthy tract, although in the main different from any other anti-Jewish work with which

I am acquainted, yet belongs with right to the general class of writings under consideration. It is divided into five sections, which are devoted to proving, chiefly from Old Testament Scripture, that Christ is the Son of God, that he is true God, that he is not a temporal but an eternal and celestial king, and that as the Jewish Messiah he has already come. The fifth section is devoted to the *ridiculæ fabulæ* of the Jews. The fourth section, which demonstrates that Christ is the Jewish Messiah, most resembles the earlier works of our class. Gen. xlix. 10 and the prophecies of Daniel play a prominent part in the demonstration, a feature which is peculiarly characteristic of the anti-Jewish works of this age.

25. Richard of St. Victor: *De Emmanuele libri duo.*
In Migne, cxcvi. 601–665. This work does not belong strictly to the class of writings under consideration, inasmuch as it has nothing to do with Scripture proofs for Christ's Messiahship. It is however written ostensibly against the Jews, and is devoted to a discussion of the Emanuel passage of Isa. vii. The work is chiefly a scholastic refutation of objections to the incarnation and related doctrines. In the second book the form of a dialogue between the author and Hugo is assumed. The work is occasioned by a commentary of "Magistri Andreæ" upon Isaiah, in which various objections of the Jews were cited, and as it appeared to Richard accepted, or at least left as insoluble. In the second book therefore Hugo is represented as one of the disciples of Andreas who adduces Jewish objections. A dialogue therefore between two Christians, instead of between a Christian and a Jew. The reason which the author gives for the adoption of the dialogistic form in the second book is interesting and significant. "Sub forma autem dialogi totam subsequentis operis seriem digessi, eo quod hic modus dicendi, vel docendi præ ceteris sit, vel ad audiendum jucundior, vel ad persuadendum efficacior. Unum itaque ex Magistri Andreæ discipulis mecum altercantem introduxi, ut sub forma ratiocinandi servata vicissitudine interrogandi et respondendi, melius elucesceret quidquid in dubium venire potuisset."

26. Petrus Blesensis: *Contra perfidiam Judæorum.*
In Migne, ccvii. 825–870. This work consists of thirty-seven chapters of "testimonies," drawn chiefly from the Old Testament. They are deduced partly in proof of various ecclesiastical doctrines, partly as prophecies of the events of Christ's life, which is treated in great detail. The last chapter contains a passage from the Sibyl-

line books, which is quoted also by Augustine in his work against the Jews, a fact noticed by the author.

27. *Tractatus sive dialogus Magistri Gualteri Tornacensis et Balduini Valentianensis contra Judæos.*

In Migne, ccix. 426-458. This work consists of three books, and is peculiar in being a dialogue between two Christians, one of whom assumes the rôle of a Jew. Bk. I. shows that the Messiah has come, by pointing out the fulfillment of prophecies in the life of Jesus. Bk. II. has considerable to say about the calling of the Gentiles, but quotes also prophecies of Christ's death, resurrection, etc. Bk. III. is wholly doctrinal, devoted chiefly to the Trinity and the Holy Spirit.

28. Alanus: *Contra hæreticos libri quattuor. Liber tertius contra Judæos.*

In Migne, ccx. 305-430. Bk. III. 400-422. The third book alone comes under consideration here. The first part of it is thoroughly scholastic, and chiefly devoted to answering objections against the Trinity urged by the Jews. The abolition of the Jewish law is then discussed, and for this many Scripture prophecies are quoted. The fact that the Messiah has already come, his divinity, his birth from the Virgin, his descent into Hades, his passion, his resurrection and ascension, are all demonstrated, chiefly from Old Testament prophecies.

29. *Tractatus adversus Judæum.*

In Martene and Durand's *Thes. nov. anecdot.* v. 1507-1568, and in Migne, ccxiii. 749-808. The first part of this anonymous tract (of the twelfth century) is a theological disquisition, which is devoted to a demonstration of the various doctrines of the church by means of proof texts drawn from Scripture. The author, in accordance with a principle laid down at the start, draws his proofs (almost) exclusively from the Old Testament, which he uses, not for prophecies, but for proof texts. In the latter part of his work, however, he dwells upon the details of Christ's life and the predictions of the Old Testament in regard to them, including the advent, birth from a virgin, Christ's coming for the nations, his passion, the destruction of Jerusalem, and the universal preaching of the Gospel. The last paragraph is devoted to the continued virginity of Mary, a subject seldom omitted in the later works of this class.

CHAPTER II.

DIALOGUE OF PAPISCUS AND PHILO.

§ 3. *Manuscripts.*

OUR dialogue is extant in three manuscripts. Of these one is in the National Library at Paris, another in the St. Mark's Library at Venice, and the third in the Library of the Most Sacred Synod at Moscow.

I. Par. Cod. Græc. 1111.[1]

The catalogue contains the following description of this manuscript:

Codex membranaceus, olim Ludovici de Targny, ibi continentur:
1. S. Johannis Damasceni de hymno trisagio epistola ad Jordanem Archimandritam. Quædam desiderantur.
2–8. Theodori Abucaræ [Seven dialogues of Theodorus Abucara, all of which are given in Migne].
9. Papisci et Jasonis Judæorum cum monacho quodam de Christiana religione et Mosaica lege colloquium.[2]
10. Colloquium aliud de non comedenda suilla, etc.
11. Theodori responsum ad objectionem sibi a Severianis propositam adversus orthodoxam fidem.
12. Ejusdem capita undecim, quibus ostenditur disparitas exempli singularis hujus hominis cum unione quæ in Christo facta est.
13. Ejusdem exemplum quo ostenditur quomodo macula peccati Adami et per incarnationem Salvatoris nostri expiatio ad universum genus humanum pervaserit.
14. Anonymus de fine mundi.
15. S. Joannis Chrys. fragmentum de eodem argumento.
16. S. Hippolyti, Episc. Romæ, opusculum de sæculi consummatione et de Antichristo.
17. S. Hieronymi interrogatio et responsa, imprimis utilia, de præcipuis religionis Christ. capitibus.

[1] This codex will be designated by the letter P.
[2] This is our dialogue, though it is given in the catalogue with an incorrect and very deceptive title.

18. Anonymi dialogus, quo ostenditur a Christianis trinitatem defendentibus Mosaïcam de Dei unitate doctrinam nec everti nec labefactari.

19. S. Joan. Dam. orthodoxæ fidei accurata expositio.

20. Ejusdem institutio elementaris ad dogmata adv. monothelitas, etc.

21. Ejusdem opusculum de duabus in Christo volentatibus et operationibus.

22. Ejusdem capita dialectica ad Cosmam.

23. Joannis orthodoxi dialogus cum Manichæo, inter Dam. opera editus.

24. Ejusdem responsio ad quæst. quare sicut dicimus humanitas Christi est ipsa humanitas Petri et Pauli, etc.

25. Ejusdem Theodori opusculum de luctatione Christi cum diabolo.

26. Interrogatio a Saraceno quodam adv. Christ. religionem proposita.

27. Ejusdem responsum ad quæst. sibi ab infidele propositam.

28. Ejusdem resp. ad quæst. sibi a Saraceno propos. Est autem dial. inter editos nonus.

29. Ejusdem dialogus adv. Nestorianum, inter ed. XIV.

30. Ejusdem dialogus adv. Nest. quo explicatur : "data est mihi omnis potestas."

31. Ejusdem dialogus tertius cum Nest., hactenus ineditus.

32. Doctrina orthodoxi, quomodo oportuit credere.

33. Exemplum libelli, sive fidei professionis a Joan. Monach. et presb. Damasceno, etc.

34. Expositio fidei quam S. Joannes Evang., jubente Maria virg., Gregorio Thaumat. revelavit.

35. Expositio parabolæ, sicut auctore S. Joan. Chrys.

36. Anonymus de quattuor formis animalium et de beatis.

Is codex sæculo duodecimo exaratus videtur.

The codex contains 244 fol. in 8vo, and dates from the eleventh or twelfth century. It is in good condition, the beginning and the end alone being somewhat worm-eaten and discolored. The page measures 18 x 13½ cm., and contains on an average 26 lines with about 32 letters to a line. There are comparatively few abbreviations, no iota subscripts and no marginal notes. The codex is written by one hand throughout. Our dialogue fills fol. 29-49.

II. Ven. Cod. Græc. 505.[1]

The catalogue describes this codex as follows : Continentur : Libanii Sophistæ epistolæ xxx. Fol. 2a–10a.
Synesii Cyrenæi epist. x. 11a–15a.
Subsequitur epist. metropolitæ cujusdam Rhodi ad metrop. Trapezuntium. 17a–24a.
Matthæi . . . patriarchæ instructio ad eos qui ad sacerdotium promoventur et ad Sacerdotes ὑπὲρ αὐτῶν μαρτυρήσοντας. 25a–31b.
Adjungitur oratio, εὐχὴ . . . 31b. ff.
Marmelis Palæologi oratio in nativitatem Christi. 33b–54b.
Nicephori Blemmydæ de imperatoris institutione . . . 57a–76b.
Disceptatio Pappisci et Philonis. 79a–87a.
Psalterium et cantica veteris et novi Testamenti, aliaque ad officium Græcorum pertinentia. 89b. ff.
In 8vo chartaceus, foliorum 375, sæculi c. xiv.

The page measures 21½ x 14 cm. and contains 28 lines, with about 40 letters to a line. The handwriting is clear, and for the most part without abbreviations. Titles and occasional capitals are in red. Our dialogue is free from marginal notes, though the remainder of the manuscript contains a great many of them. In 1868, a student in the library disfigured the codex by adding nonsensical titles to various works. Our dialogue is absurdly designated : Φλαβίου Ἰοσέφου Ἰησός.

III. The third manuscript, which is in the Bibliotheca Sanctissimæ Synodi at Moscow[2] (Cod. Græc. $\frac{314}{cccl}$) is described by Matthæi as follows[3] : Codex in charta bombycina sec. xv. foliorum 146. Fuit antea in monasterio Iberorum. A principio est mutilus. Continet collectionem canonum, Rhodiorum νόμον ναυτικὸν et ἀντιβολὴν Παπίσκου καὶ Φίλωνος Ἰουδαίων πρὸς μοναχὸν περὶ πίστεως χριστιανῶν.[4] Ejus initium : "ἠρώτησεν Παπίσκος ὁ Ἰουδαῖος, διατί τοῦ Θεοῦ παραγγέλοντος."

[1] This codex will be designated by the letter V.
[2] This codex will be designated by the letter M.
[3] I owe my knowledge of this codex to a communication made to Professor Adolf Harnack by Dr. Oscar von Gebhardt. I have not been able to examine the codex myself, but the librarian in Moscow has very kindly furnished me with its variant readings for the first three pages of the dialogue, which commences at fol. 131.
[4] Matthæi does not give the title fully, as will be seen by a comparison of the text, where the variations of M are given.

§ 4. *Relation between the Two Forms of the Dialogue.*

The two manuscripts of our dialogue, P and V, give recensions of the work differing greatly in extent as well as in many minor details. It takes but a casual examination to convince any one that the recension represented by V is older than that represented by P, although the former manuscript is at least two centuries younger than the latter. The most obvious evidence of this is the fact that the recension represented by P (which we shall call RP for brevity's sake) expressly indicates the date of its composition as the eleventh century, while the recension represented by V (RV) as clearly indicates the seventh or eighth. This is in itself decisive proof of the later date of RP, unless it be supposed that the numbers were inserted by some mere copyist and are independent of the respective recensions as a whole. Such a conclusion could of course be accepted only under the pressure of strong internal grounds. Let us then compare the two forms somewhat in detail to ascertain whether the relation indicated by the dates is borne out by internal evidence. For the later origin of RP speak the following arguments:

1. The passage inserted by P (after Μαρίας, p. 53, 1. 13), which is omitted by both V and An.,[1] is clearly a later interpolation, for there is no connection between it and the answer of the Jew which follows. The latter is evidently to be connected directly with 1. 13.

2. The passage which in P follows ἐβασίλευσεν (p. 58, l. 7) seems to be a later insertion, for we can see otherwise no reason for its omission both by V and An. It may be noticed too that the use of ὁ Δαβὶδ at the beginning is peculiar. If all were the work of one hand we should expect simply καὶ πάλιν. Again the phrase διαρρήδην φάσκει used in connection with Malachi is suspicious, for neither of these words occurs again in the whole work.

3. The most important difference between the two forms occurs in the passage upon the details of Christ's life, p. 65 ff. The fuller and more highly developed form of P appears at once to be later than the very simple form of V. If however it be suggested that V has simply omitted the fuller particulars of P for the sake of brevity (a thing very improbable in itself, since this passage forms the strongest part of the Christian's argument) it can be shown that

---

[1] The abbreviation An. is used to designate the work of Anastasius, mentioned above, p. 17, whose relations to our dialogue are discussed below, p. 35 ff.

internal indications confirm the later insertion of the passages peculiar to P. We need mention but two points. First, the use of ἀκούσωμεν in introducing quotations. This form occurs ten times in the passage in question, and only once in the rest of the work, and that in introducing one of the Daniel quotations which is likewise peculiar to P; so that V does not once have the form.

A second and decisive point is the difference in the wording of Isa. ix. 6 as quoted on p. 57 in the part of the work common to both MSS. and on p. 66 in the part peculiar to P. The writer of RP certainly used a LXX. text different from that used by the writer of the original of the earlier portion of the dialogue, while in copying that earlier portion he simply transcribed his source directly as it stood.

4. P contains a long passage (p. 80 ff.) which is devoted chiefly to prophecies from Daniel, and is wholly omitted by V. The very nature of this passage, which is so different from the rest of the work, excites suspicion at once. Again, the same form ἀκούσωμεν, which occurs elsewhere only in the long passage mentioned as peculiar to P, occurs once in this portion of the work. And finally, not to multiply arguments for so patent a fact, this whole passage is omitted not only by V but also by An., which contains otherwise much that is peculiar to P over against V. Other minor additions of P which witness to a later hand will be mentioned in the notes.

We conclude then that RV is certainly older than RP.

The question then arises, did RP draw directly from RV or must we assume an older common source? Although the variations between V and P are numerous, they are nevertheless of such a character as to furnish no reason for assuming an older common source, and more than that V contains no passage of any length omitted by P, so that the original cannot at any rate have differed in extent from RV. And when it is remembered that V is two centuries later than P, the variations, all of which are but minor, are easily explained. We may look upon RV then as the original of RP.[1]

§ 5. *Relation of the Dialogue to other Anti-Jewish Works.*

An interesting question connected with our dialogue is its relation to other works of the kind.

---

[1] That RP used another source in addition to RV will be shown in § 5.

Its title leads us at once to look for some relationship between it and the lost dialogue of Papiscus and Jason. But in this expectation we find ourselves disappointed. Our actual knowledge of that ancient dialogue is very limited; at the same time we know enough about it to be able to conclude that the present work stands in no literary relationship to it.

Harnack, in his most keen and suggestive essay already mentioned, has summed up [1] the facts known in regard to the contents of the lost work under thirteen heads. Our dialogue was probably composed in Egypt (see below, § 7), where the dialogue of Papiscus and Jason was well known, and to which country Papiscus was represented as belonging. Again the older dialogue treated chiefly of Christ, and was devoted to showing that the Old Testament Messianic prophecies correspond to the facts of Jesus' life. In both of these points our dialogue agrees well with the lost one; but the agreement ceases here. The latter belonged to the class of works which contain allegories; it concluded with the conversion of the Jew; Deut. xxi. 23 was quoted, and that in the form given by Aquila; Gen. i. 1 was interpreted as if it read: "In filio fecit Deus cœlum et terram;" the expression "seven heavens" was found in it; the dialogue was perhaps of an apocalyptic nature. Of all these characteristic traits not one appears in our present dialogue, a series of omissions exceedingly difficult to explain if the writer based his work in any way upon the earlier one. The title, which so strongly suggests the older dialogue, will be discussed below (§ 6).

The next point is to inquire whether our dialogue shows any relationship to Justin's Dialogue with Trypho. Such a relationship might appear in itself antecedently probable, as Justin's work was widely circulated and enjoyed a very high reputation.[2] But a comparison of the two works shows no connection between them. They exhibit an entirely different line of thought, different interpretations of Biblical passages which they happen to have in common, and all that is most characteristic of Justin's dialogue is lacking in the present one. To attempt a detailed exhibition of the differences would be useless. Justin's dialogue contains about 385 Old Testament quotations and the dialogue of Papiscus and Philo about 103. Of these but 38 are common to both works, and most of them are used in different connections, and many of them

---

[1] *Texte und Untersuchungen*, Bd. I. Heft 3, p. 116 ff.
[2] We know too that it was used by Tertullian in his *Adv. Judæos*.

interpreted in a manner quite unlike in the two. A resemblance between the two occurs in the application of the words of Psa. lxxi. 1, to Solomon both by Trypho (c. 34) and by Papiscus-Philo (p. 55); but the language in the two cases is quite different, and the application of the words to Solomon is too natural to need any literary dependence to explain it. Another resemblance is found between Trypho, c. 49 and Pap., p. 56, where the Jews avow their expected Messiah to be only human; but of this the same may be said.

Harnack has shown that a common source (probably the dialogue of Papiscus and Jason) existed, of which Tertullian, Cyprian, Lactantius and Evagrius made extensive use, and which explains their common and often striking agreement in a portion of their Biblical citations. But our dialogue shows no more of a connection with these works than with the dialogues of Papiscus and Jason, and of Justin and Trypho. Further its independence of the assumed common source is still more marked, for the passages common to it and to that source reduce themselves to seven in number, and in these the resemblance is in no case striking. Cyprian's *Testimonia*, the fullest development of this common type, was widely used among occidental writers subsequent to his time (see Harnack, *ib.* p. 97 ff.). But in the orient we find no trace of a knowledge of the work (in itself of course antecedently improbable), and what is still more important, no trace of a use of the common source from which the various occidental writers drew. The Pseudo-Gregorian *Testimonia adv. Judæos* (a work very similar in scope and character to the *Testimonia* of Cyprian), Chrysostom's *Adversus Judæos*, the dialogue of Gregentius with Herbano the Jew, and our own dialogue, although all devote a large space to the fulfillment of prophecy in the life of Christ, yet are all quite independent of the source mentioned, and at the same time of each other. The resemblances to be sure between the Pseudo-Gregorian *Testimonia* and our dialogue are a little more marked than those between the latter and the *Testimonia* of Cyprian (of the particulars in regard to the life of Christ contained in Pseudo-Gregory all are found in RP, though the texts cited are often quite different), and yet not sufficiently so to warrant the assumption of any literary connection. A common tradition grown into a habit of pointing out certain coincidences between prophecy and the life of Christ seems enough to account for all the resemblances, and we are thus enabled at the same time to explain the differences, both in the details mentioned and in the texts quoted, differences which are very numerous and very great between all these works. Each writer meanwhile in pointing out new details would add to the common stock of material upon this subject, of which we should expect later writers to make use. It is therefore not surprising that RP should contain the details of Pseudo-Gregory and of other works. The great differences in the texts quoted, in the details themselves (Gregory containing many others on the Sacraments, circumcision, the Sabbath, etc., entirely omitted by Papiscus), in the general arrangement and plan of the two works utterly preclude any direct literary dependence. The resemblance between our dialogue and the works of Chrysostom and of Gregentius is still less.

A work is extant however which is very closely connected with our dialogue. This is the work (or rather collection of works, for it contains five separate tracts) which bears the title 'Αναστασίου ἀββᾶ διάλεξις κατὰ 'Ιουδαίων (no. 19 in the list of Greek works given in § 2). Large portions of this work are identical with the dialogue of Papiscus and Philo. The question at once confronts us, how are the two related ? Is our dialogue a mere extract from the larger work, or is the latter an enlargement of the former, or do the two spring from an older source ?

The first supposition is ruled out by the respective dates of the two works. RV belongs to the seventh or eighth centuries (see § 7), while Anastasius' work belongs to the ninth. These dates, which are distinctly given in the writings themselves, we have no reason to doubt, especially since a comparison of RV and An. shows that the former contains every mark of originality over against the latter. At the same time, that An. is not itself an original work is antecedently probable, both from its fragmentary character and from the fact that it purports to be simply a collection of directions how to answer a Jew in case he makes certain objections or asks certain questions. The probability is further confirmed by the irregularity of construction in introducing the objections of the Jew. Sometimes they are given in direct discourse, sometimes in indirect, a course which is best explained by supposing the writer to have drawn from a source which had the form of a dialogue and to have been careless in his reproduction of it. A decisive proof of the non-original character of An. lies in the opening sentence of the second tract, which begins καὶ γὰρ ἅπαντα. The previous tract had closed with a doxology, and was thus quite complete in itself. The καὶ γάρ of the opening sentence of the second shows clearly that it is simply an extract from a previous work torn abruptly from its context. The exact words occur, in fact, in RV in their proper connection.

On the other hand, nothing which RV contains is omitted by An., except the external setting of the dialogue, which, of course, was dropped when the dialogistic form was given up. This leads us to conclude that the source of An. was practically identical with RV; that is, that no common source for the two need be assumed.[1]

But a comparison of An. with the fuller form RP reveals connections between the two which cannot be explained by their common use of RV. An. in many places agrees with RV in the omission of passages which RP contains, but at the same time it has a great deal in common with RP over against RV. On the other hand, RV and RP agree in many points over against An., notably in the title, in the first paragraph, and in the dialogistic form with all its accessories. In any case therefore, RV lies at the base of both, and neither can be explained by its exclusive use of the other. Meanwhile, the respective dates of An. and RP rule out the dependence of the former upon the latter. There remain, therefore, but two possibilities open : either RP made use of An. in addition to RV, or both RP and An. made use of a common work which included RV, that is, was a later growth from it. In the latter case of course the dependence of An. and RP upon RV is not direct but mediate. Meanwhile, inasmuch as P has every one of the prophetic particulars contained in An. and with a similarity of language which involves literary connection in all of them, the source from which RP drew must have contained them all. But it is noticeable that in An. they are given, a part of them in the second treatise, a part in the third, and, when compared with RP, in a very disordered way. It is impossible to conceive that An. could in the second treatise have omitted entirely so many of these particulars and in the third have introduced them in so different an order if the source contained them as given in RP. This of course confirms the fact, which we have already accepted as established by the respective dates, that An. did not draw from RP (a fact further confirmed by its much less full and developed form in respect to these particulars), and also goes to show that An., in addition to the common source RV,

[1] Upon the "Anastasius" of the two titles, see below, § 6.

cannot have drawn from another source any more like RP than itself.

Further it is a significant fact that on p. 69, l. 8, RP shows its dependence upon a non-dialogistic source, for it reads ἐρώτησον λοιπὸν τὸν Ἰουδαῖον καὶ εἰπὲ αὐτῷ, which is evidently a reminiscence of a work of the same nature as An. in which this sort of phrase occurs frequently. It is true that RP varies considerably from An. in detail, and that it omits entirely a great deal which An. contains. But in the variations RP is almost always superior to An., both in arrangement and in logical force, and they can thus be easily explained as purposed improvements upon the part of the former. In regard to the long passages omitted, we have no right to expect that RP would transcribe the whole of An. The writer took naturally only such parts as he wished, and those were especially the sections containing the detailed prophecies of Christ's life, of which he adopted every one, gathering them from the different parts of An. and arranging them in a logical and symmetrical way. From the omission of the lengthy discussion of An. upon the history of the Jews and justification by faith and works, we have no right to assume a lack of knowledge of them on the part of RP.

We may conclude then that there exists nothing to necessitate the assumption of a common source for An. and RP over and above RV, but that all the phenomena are explained by supposing RP to have made use of both RV and An.[1] This conclusion agrees exactly with what the respective dates of the works would lead us to expect.

§ 6. *Sources and Title.*

The reader must be struck, upon the most hasty perusal, with the utter lack of connection between the first paragraph of our dialogue and that which follows. It cannot be supposed that the author began his work with this utterly foreign passage upon image

---

[1] It is noticeable that An. and RP have nothing in common which is omitted by RV except in connection with the details of Christ's life. Aside from these details both seem to have drawn directly from RV, and RP seems to have paid no attention to An. If this fact were pressed, it might appear to lead to the assumption of a common source for An. and RP, containing the dialogistic setting and all the common peculiarities of RV and RP over against An., while at the same time enlarged in the direction of An. so as to include all the details upon Christ's life found in the latter, and in the same order as in it. The assumption of such a source would account fully for RP without supposing a direct dependence on its part upon either RV or An. In this case the minor verbal

worship, and then passed over so abruptly to the subject which constitutes the substance of the dialogue. The only possible explanation of the matter, if a single author be assumed for the whole, is the addition of this passage after the completion of the body of the work, for the purpose of attracting interest in an age when the image controversy was absorbing all minds. But against this speak two very obvious facts. First, the reference to images on p. 75 presupposes the existence of this introductory passage, and secondly, the Christian is called in the opening paragraph μοναχὸς by V, and ἀββᾶς by P, while in the remainder of the work he is uniformly called χριστιανὸς by both MSS. We are thus led to conclude that the opening paragraph is the addition of a later hand, and, if this paragraph, then also the passage upon the same subject on p. 75. RV is therefore not the original form of our dialogue. But when we ask what was the original form, we can frame only a conjectural answer. The passages which have been shown to be later additions of P, and the paragraphs just mentioned are of course to be stricken out, but further than that we cannot go with certainty. Other passages which it seems probable did not belong to the original will be referred to in the notes.

The question next arises, what was the title of the original source which has been shown to have existed? In turning to this question we are met by a peculiar fact. In our existing title two Jews are mentioned, while in the dialogue itself only one is represented as speaking. It is certain that the title and the dialogue as they stand cannot be from the same hand, and it is further certain that the singular form of the text is older than the plural form of the title, for no one would have changed Ἰουδαῖοι throughout to Ἰουδαῖος, while leaving the title in the plural.[1] When and how

agreements of An. and RP over against RV (in the sections common also to RV) might represent the altered form of the intermediate source. Still facts do not necessitate the existence of such a source, and we may therefore rest content with the conclusion reached above, that RP drew directly from RV and An. In that case the minor verbal agreements just spoken of, representing as they would the form of RV used by both An. and RP, would be a stronger witness to the original form than the later manuscript V. It has seemed best however to give the text according to V rather than to introduce conjectural emendations.

[1] Ἰουδαῖοι occurs once in P, p. 56, l. 22 (where V has the singular), but this is owing to the multitude of Jews who are mentioned shortly before as onlookers, and has no reference to the two Jews of the title. The plural occurs once also in V, p. 65, l. 6. See note on p. 89.

then did the plural form arise ? Did the original title contain the names of the two contesting parties—of a Jew and a Christian—or did it simply contain the name of the author (as the dialogues of Petrus Damianus, of Gilbert of Westminster, etc.), or no name at all (as the anonymous Latin dialogue in Migne, clxiii. 1015 ff.) ? The first alternative is antecedently the most probable, when the analogy of similar works is considered,[1] and this probability is strengthened, as we shall see, by the existing form. Our title as it stands arouses at first sight the suspicion that the names Papiscus and Philo have been added as representative Jews, typical of the Jewish people as a whole, the former name being naturally suggested for such a dialogue from its use in the earlier dialogue of Papiscus and Jason, the latter as the name of the great Jewish philosopher. In this case the original title either contained no Jewish name (for we cannot suppose an original name to have been displaced to make room for two others), or it contained one and the other was afterward added. If the former was the case it is difficult to explain the addition of two names when the dialogue itself runs throughout in the singular, and still more so to explain the name Papiscus, which stands in the opening of V and M without Philo. This latter fact seems to indicate that Papiscus stood originally in the title and Philo was afterwards added, but it is difficult to see the necessity for such an addition both inconsistent with the dialogue itself and out of all analogy with other works of the kind. The simplest explanation of the matter seems to me to be that the original title contained both names, Papiscus and Philo, but that the former only was the name of a Jew, the latter the name of a Christian. We should then have to think of the title as bearing the form Ἀντιβολὴ Παπίσκου καὶ Φίλωνος, which would agree excellently with the titles of other anti-Jewish dialogues. The name Papiscus then might represent an actual Jew, or be simply a repetition of the name used in the dialogue of Papiscus and Jason. The latter is of course much more probable, for that two Jews should have existed in different ages and both separately either actually have taken part in or have been represented as taking part in dialogues with Jews is quite improbable, especially when we realize the uncommonness of the name, for, so far as the writer knows, the name occurs nowhere else than in these two

[1] Cf. Ἰάσονος καὶ Παπίσκου ἀντιλογία περὶ Χριστοῦ, *Altercatio Simonis et Theophili*, etc.

dialogues. It is therefore probable that the author owes the name Papiscus to the earlier dialogue, which we know was still in circulation in the seventh century, for it is mentioned by Maximus Confessor.[1] It is of course not necessary to conclude that the author had himself read the earlier dialogue, though the lack of all resemblance between the two works cannot be urged as absolutely proving that he had not.

The name Philo then might either have been taken from some prominent Christian of the age (we know of a number of Christian Philos of the fourth and following centuries), or it might have been the name of the author himself. This being the original title of the dialogue, it is very easy to explain the later corruption. When the Christian Philo meant in the title had dropped out of memory, it would be quite natural to think, in connection with this name, of the great Jewish philosopher, and later editors or copyists would then have before them the singular spectacle of an anti-Jewish dialogue held between two Jews. The extension of the title, when it was once thus interpreted, became of course a necessity. There is a hint of this subsequent extension in the designation of the Christian which occurs in the extant title. P and M give no name to him, but call him simply μοναχόν τινα, a most remarkably impersonal designation if it be a part of the original title. Its later addition however is quite natural. The editor who added it thought, very likely, that the original name of the Christian had fallen out, and instead of inserting presumptuously a particular name, for which he had no authority, he simply subjoined "with a certain monk," for that the dialogue must have been with *some* Christian was self-evident.

That the name Ἀναστάσιος of V is a later addition seems probable for two reasons: first, because we can otherwise see no ground for its omission by both P and M, which are otherwise independent of each other (so far as can be judged from the brief extract of M which has been compared); secondly, because of the occurrence of τινα in connection with the Ἀναστάσιον of V. When there existed a reason for adding the name Anastasius, which could have been only because of his prominence as a Christian, or because he himself revised the dialogue, it would have been peculiar to call him "a certain monk, Anastasius." In fact, it seems clear that the μοναχόν τινα of P, M and V was the original addition, and

[1] See Harnack: *Texte und Untersuchungen*, Bd. I. Heft I. p. 123.

that later the "Anastasius" of V was attached. We have further a hint as to the origin of this name. The Abbot Anastasius, in the work mentioned in § 5, as shown there makes extensive use of our dialogue, incorporating into his larger work almost the whole of it as it exists in V, and at the same time dropping the dialogistic form. He wrote in the ninth century. It would be very natural for his name, some centuries later, to be commonly connected with the dialogue itself which he had worked over, and all the more so since that represented the Christian as a monk and yet left his personality entirely indefinite. Thus it is not in the least unlikely that the writer of the manuscript V, of the fourteenth century, added Anastasius' name to the impersonal designation which existed in his copy. This may of course have been done in all good faith, and the manuscript may in other respects have been exactly like its original.

The word $\mu o \nu a \chi \acute{o} s$ occurs both in the title and in the first paragraph of the dialogue ($\dot{a}\beta\beta\tilde{a}s$ in P) and nowhere else. It is therefore natural, though of course not necessary, to conclude that the two additions are from the same hand, that the person who revised the original dialogue enlarged the original title. The addition we can easily understand. It was done in a time when the image controversy was raging, that is, not before the sixth century, nor yet later than the seventh (for RV dates from the beginning of the eighth, or from the end of the seventh century). The redactor wished to fit the dialogue to the age and took the easiest way to do it. A work could not expect much of a circulation at that time unless it touched upon the great question of the day. It was a capital way too to depict the Christianity of image worship by picturing its opponent as a Jew, and an effective "tract for the times" was thus produced with a minimum of labor. The insertion of the word $\mu o \nu a \chi \acute{o} s$ was likewise most natural. It carried weight with it in those days and meant far more than the simple $\chi \rho \iota \sigma \tau \iota a \nu \acute{o} s$. The monks, too, were the great champions of image worship.

§ 7. *Time and Place of Composition. Authorship.*

Having thus reached probable conclusions as to the source and title of our work, we may finally inquire as to its authorship, and the time and place of its composition.

The date of each of our recensions is given with considerable exactness. On p. 65 RV, in speaking of the words of Christ, says ἅπερ πρὸ ἑξακοσίων ἐτῶν προεῖπεν. On p. 78 the Jews are said to have been driven about the world for 600 years, and in the following sentence the destruction of Jerusalem under Vespasian and Titus is mentioned, which would seem to imply that these years are to be reckoned from 70 A.D. These figures therefore, taken as round numbers, would bring us down to the seventh century. But on p. 79 the Jews are said to have been without sacrifices, without the passover, etc., for 670 years. It seems impossible to bring this number into harmony with the two preceding. If it be counted from 70 A.D. it brings us to the year 740, and if that be the true date we should expect on p. 65 to find ἑπτακοσίων ἐτῶν instead of ἑξακοσίων, it being to the author's interest to make the time as long as possible. The most probable explanation of the difficulty seems to be that the writer in the present instance reckoned from the destruction of Jerusalem under Hadrian; for although this destruction is not spoken of in the context, yet, correctly speaking, he could count the complete abolition of sacrifices only from that date. In that case he must have written πεντακόσια ἑβδομήκοντα instead of ἑξακόσια ἑβδομήκοντα, and some copyist, having already written ἑξακόσια twice, wrote it again in this case by mistake. If this explanation be the true one the writer of RV was more conscientious in his reckoning than the writers of An. and RP, who count in both cases from the destruction of Jerusalem under Titus. We are thus led to assign the composition of RV to the very end of the seventh century or to the beginning of the eighth.[1]

The same passages in An., meanwhile, substitute for the figures of RV on p. 65 πρὸ χρόνων ὀκτακοσίων ἢ καὶ ἐπέκεινα, and for the figures on pp. 73 and 79 ὀκτακόσια καὶ πλείονα. The inexactness of the statement does not permit us to fix the date with precision; we can simply say toward the end of the ninth century. The writer in the present case clearly reckoned both on p. 78 and on p. 79 from 70 A.D.

RP meanwhile substitutes for the numbers of RV and of An. on pp. 78 and 79 the number 1000. On p. 65 it has simply the indefinite expression πολλῶν ἐτῶν, but on p. 61 (note 84) it contains another datum, which is omitted by RV and An. The last, taken

[1] It cannot have been as late as 730, for then on p. 65 we should find 700 instead of 600.

with preciseness, would lead us to about the year 1030; but taken as a round number, as it is evidently meant to be taken, it is in substantial harmony with the figures of pp. 78 and 79, which point to about the year 1070 for the composition of RP.

A more exact date may perhaps be drawn from another passage in RP. On p. 61 (note 3) occur the words μὴ γάρ μοι τοῦτο σκοπήσητε ἢ εἴπητε ὅτι ἄρτι εἰς τὰ κ΄ ταῦτα ἔτη παιδευόμεϑα οἱ χριστιανοὶ κ.τ.λ. The interpretation of the sentence is somewhat dark, but it seems to imply that the Christians had been undergoing some sort of a persecution for twenty years. It is probable, as will be shown below, that our dialogue was written in Egypt, and it happens to be a fact that about the year 1058 under the Caliph El-Mustansir a persecution broke out in Alexandria against the Christians. We know of no other at about this time to which the author could have referred, and the agreement in the present case is quite remarkable. The internal relations of the three forms confirm this order of composition, as we have already shown, and there is therefore no reason to doubt the accuracy of these dates.

A more interesting question is as to the date of the original lost source. Here we are left entirely to conjecture. There is nothing in it except the passing reference to the eternal virginity of Mary, which would prevent a very early date. At the same time the absence of later doctrines in a work of this class is not a decisive proof of its antiquity, as has been shown in Chap. I., § 1. The *terminus a quo* is given by the words ἀεὶ παρϑένου applied to Mary,[1] words which could not have been used before the fifth century. The *terminus ad quem* is given by the date of RV, namely, the early part of the eighth century or end of the seventh. Meanwhile, if our view of the form of the original title be correct, considerable time must have elapsed between its composition and its use by RV, and still further its omission of all reference to image worship, which it was found necessary to insert in the later recensions, would likewise seem to point to a date nearer the beginning than the end of the period mentioned.

As to the place of composition a hint is furnished us by the enumeration of the various religious cults on p. 74. Nearly all of them are Egyptian, a fact which points strongly to the Egyptian

---

[1] Unless the possibility that the whole phrase is a later insertion, as suggested in the notes, be accepted, in which case there is nothing in the dialogue to prevent a much earlier date.

origin of the work. Again the persecution mentioned above fits so well, as far as date is concerned, that it is allowable to urge this agreement as an additional testimony to the Egyptian origin of RP. If this be accepted for our three recensions the most natural conclusion is that the original source was also of Egyptian origin.

As to the authorship of RV and of RP we have no clue (the Anastasius of RV being, as already shown, a later addition). An. purports to be the work of an abbot Anastasius, and we have no reason to question this. It cannot of course be the work of Anastasius Sinaiticus (although it is printed among his writings by Migne), for it is some centuries too late for him. Nor can it be the work of Anastasius, Abbot of St. Eutimius in Palestine, as supposed by others, for he lived in the early part of the eighth century, not in the ninth. There is in fact no ground for connecting the work with any particular Anastasius known to us. The name was a very common one and the compilation may perhaps be the work of an Anastasius of whom we know nothing.

As to the authorship of the original source we are of course left entirely to conjecture. It has been, however, suggested above that the Philo of the title may be the name of the original author; we know of a number of Christians of this name of the fourth and following centuries,[1] and the work may have been written by one of them or by some other Philo unknown to us.

§ 8. *Analysis of the Dialogue.*

The dialogue dispenses with a formal introduction and opens abruptly with a question from the Jew. If the first paragraph, which is quite independent of the remainder of the dialogue, be left out of consideration for the moment, the work consists of three general sections. The first extends from p. 52 to p. 65, and is devoted in the main to the divine sonship and pre-existence of Christ, as proved by the predictions of the Old Testament. The second [2] (pp. 65 to 73) contains an account of the life of Jesus, which is shown to have been foretold in detail by the prophets. These two divisions are thus chiefly biblical. The third (pp. 73 to 80) is devoted in the main to an exhibition of the prosperity of Christianity in contrast with the fall of heathendom, and especially

---

[1] Cf. the list given by Fabricius-Harles, iv. 750 ff.
[2] This is very brief in V, but carried out in great detail by P.

the misfortunes of the Jews—an argument, therefore, for the truth of Christianity drawn from history. § 17 (pp. 80 to 82), which is wholly wanting in the Venetian manuscript, may be regarded as a separate section, or simply as a biblical supplement to the historical argument of the third division. The work is supplemented (in the Paris MS.) with a formal conclusion stating the reason for its composition.

We may divide the whole for convenience's sake into seventeen paragraphs.

§ 1. The work opens with a question from the Jew, who asks why the Christians worship images when such worship has been forbidden by God. The Christian answers that they do not worship the images themselves, but through them Christ.

§ 2. The Jew, without expressing satisfaction or dissatisfaction with the answer of the Christian, passes abruptly to another subject, inquiring why the Christians blaspheme by saying that God has a son. The Christian proceeds to show that this is taught in the Jewish Scriptures, beginning his proof with the familiar passage, Psa. ii. 7. The Jew claims that this refers to Solomon, an opinion which the Christian demonstrates to be untenable.

§ 3. The Jew then asks how God can say, "Ask of me," as if speaking to a servant, if the person addressed be his son. He inquires also how the words, "This day have I begotten thee," can be reconciled with the Christian doctrine of the pre-existence of Christ. The first trivial objection the Christian disposes of briefly, and answers the second by applying the words of the psalm to the birth according to the flesh.

§ 4. The Jew considers it impossible that Christ, if born of Mary, could have existed before the world, and be God. The Christian then proposes to show from the Jewish Scriptures and the prophets the truth of what the Christians preach concerning Christ.

§ 5. He begins by showing that the "Son was begotten of the Father before all creation."

§ 6. He then asks the Jew whether the Messiah expected by them is to be God or mere man. The Jew replies that he is to be a mere man, like one of the prophets.

§ 7. The Christian upon this appeals to the spectators and proposes that the Scriptures be examined, and if they have proclaimed the coming Messiah to be God, then the Christ worshiped by the Christians is truly God and Christ, but the one whom the Jews expect is a deceiver and Antichrist ; while on the other hand if the prophets are not shown to have proclaimed the Messiah as God, then the Christians are deceived and the Jews speak the truth. He therefore causes them to bring their books from their synagogue, and proposes to draw his proofs from them.

§ 8. He begins by quoting numerous passages from the Psalms and prophets to prove that Christ is God.

§ 9. He then proceeds to show that the Messiah was promised as the Messiah of the nations. Quoting among other passages Jacob's blessing upon Judah (Gen. xlix. 10) he points out that the terms of the prophecy have been already fulfilled, since the Jews have no longer king, rulers, temple, etc. Their sacred places have all been taken from them and given to the Christians, whose name is spread everywhere in spite of the many persecutions which they have suffered.

§ 10. He then puts the question : If Christianity be false, why has God preserved it so wonderfully in the face of such enemies ? The church endures but its adversaries have perished. In this connection he shows that the prophecies of Christ himself have been proved true, quoting a number of them and pointing out their fulfillment in detail.

§ 11. The Jew then asks why, if it were true, the prophets did not clearly foretell that Christ should come and do away with the Jewish ritual. The Christian answers that they would have been stoned had they thus prophesied, and their books would have been burned, which would have been a great loss to the Christians, for even now, he says, he has been able to refute the Jew from those very books.

§ 12. This leads him to return to the prophets, and he proceeds to make extracts from them which foretell the life of Christ in detail. In V four, in P thirty-five separate particulars of his life are mentioned, covering the time from his advent to his ascension. From this paragraph on the Jew says nothing and the work thus loses entirely the dialogistic form.

§ 13. The Christian concludes this section upon the details of Christ's life by asking, Who can deny Christ to be true God after hearing all this, for the Christians hold him to be not a mere man, but God incarnate who has overthrown idols and destroyed the sacrifices of demons ? This leads him to inquire what has become of the priests of Memphis, of the worship of the Nile, etc., and to draw the contrast between their obliteration and the prosperity of Christianity.

§ 14. After his long digression he returns to the question of the Jew, as to why the prophets had not foretold the doing away of the Jewish ritual, and meets it by inquiring in return why the prophets had not foretold that a false Christ would come calling himself Jesus.

§ 15. He then goes back to the first question of the Jew in regard to the Christians' worship of images, and retorts by inquiring why the Jews worshiped the image of Nebuchadnezzar and the golden calf. This leads him to dwell upon their faithlessness and blindness, and to quote various Old Testament passages denunciatory of their wickedness.

§ 16. As a consequence of their sins the Jews were sent in captivity to Babylon, but after seventy years were restored to their own country. What sin did they then commit of such magnitude as to cause God again to destroy their city and to banish them from it, this time for so many centuries? If they will not answer, the very stones will cry out that it is because they crucified Christ.

At this point the work comes to an end in V, and a doxology is added.[1]

§ 17 (in P) gives extended quotations from Daniel, in which the destruction of Jerusalem, the dispersion of the Jews, and the coming of the Messiah are foretold, and the work proper is brought to a close with a doxology.

The writer then adds that he has made these quotations from the prophets in order to confirm the faith of the Christians, and to convict the Jews. He concludes with an exhortation to fulfill the commands of Christ in return for the salvation accomplished by him, and in order to obtain the blessings of eternity.

[1] The second tract of An. also ends at the same point.

THE TEXT.

ABBREVIATIONS.

V   = Ven. Cod. Græc. 505.

P   = Par. Cod. Græc. 1111.

M   = Bibl. Mosq. Sanct. Synodi Cod. Græc. $\frac{314}{CCCI}$.

An. = Anastasii Abbatis adv. Judæos disputatio.

THE text is given according to V except in the few places where V is manifestly incorrect, when P and An. are followed. All the variations of P of every description are given. The variations of M are given so far as known, that is for the first two pages. The variations of An. from the text of V are given wherever the two texts run parallel, but not its variations from P in the long passage which V omits, for P and An. are so different at this point, both in matter and arrangement, as to preclude the possibility of such comparison.

ΑΝΤΙΒΟΛΗ ΠΑΠΙΣΚΟΥ[1] ΚΑΙ ΦΙΛΩΝΟΣ ΙΟΥΔΑΙΩΝ ΤΩΝ ΠΑΡ ΕΒΡΑΙΟΙΣ ΣΟΦΩΝ ΠΡΟΣ ΜΟΝΑΧΟΝ ΤΙΝΑ[2] ΠΕΡΙ ΠΙΣΤΕΩΣ ΧΡΙΣΤΙΑΝΩΝ ΚΑΙ ΝΟΜΟΥ ΕΒΡΑΙΩΝ[3] ΚΡΟΤΗΘΕΙΣΑ ΕΠΙ ΔΗΜΟΥ ΧΡΙΣΤΙΑΝΩΝ[4] ΚΑΙ ΙΟΥΔΑΙΩΝ. 5

1. Ἠρώτησε[1] Παπίσκος[2] Ἰουδαῖος·[3] διὰ τί τοῦ θεοῦ παραγγέλοντος[4] μὴ προσκυνεῖν λίθον ἢ ξύλον,[5] ὑμεῖς ταῦτα σέβεσθε καὶ προσκυνεῖτε ποιοῦντες ἐξ αὐτῶν σταυροὺς καὶ εἰκόνας; ἀπεκρίθην ὁ μοναχός·[6] εἰπέ μοι σύ,[7] διὰ τί ὁ Ἰακὼβ 10 προσεκύνησε τὸ ἄκρον τῆς ῥάβδου τοῦ Ἰωσήφ;[a] ὁ Ἰουδαῖος εἶπεν·[8] οὐχὶ τὴν ῥάβδον προσεκύνησεν ἢ τὸ ξύλον, ἀλλὰ τὸν κρατοῦντα αὐτὴν[9] Ἰωσὴφ ἐτίμησεν. ὁ μοναχὸς[10] εἶπεν·[11] οὕτως καὶ ἡμεῖς προσκυνοῦντες τὸν σταυρόν, οὐ τὴν φύσιν τοῦ ξύλου προσκυνοῦμεν· 15 μὴ γένοιτο· ἀλλὰ τὸν σταυρωθέντα ἐν αὐτῷ. καὶ ὥσπερ σὺ προσκυνεῖς[12] εἰ[13] εὕρῃς[14] τὰς δύο πλάκας καὶ τὰ δύο χερουβὶμ ἅπερ ἐποίησε Μωϋσῆς, καὶ τὴν κιβωτόν, τιμῶν τὸν θεὸν τὸν ἐπιτάξαντα αὐτά,[15] οὕτω κἀγὼ προσκυνῶν τὰς εἰκόνας, οὐ τὸ ξύλον προσ- 20 κυνῶ·[16] μὴ γένοιτο·[17] ἀλλὰ τὸν Χριστὸν τιμῶν καὶ τοὺς ἁγίους αὐτοῦ.

καὶ[18] ὅτι οὔτε[19] τὸ ξύλον οὔτε[20] τὴν ζωγραφίαν προσκυνῶ, ἐκ τούτου[21] δῆλον, ὅτι πολλάκις τὰς εἰκόνας

[1] Παπίσκου PM, Παππίσκου V.
[2] Ἀναστάσιον add. V ; om. PM.
[3] Ἑβραίων V, ἑβραικοῦ PM.
[4] Ἀρράβων τε add. P, Ἀράβων τε add. M.
[1] Ἠρώτησεν M.
[2] Παππίσκος V.
[3] Ἐρώτημα Ἰουδαίου P.
[4] παραγγελόντος P, παραγγείλαντος An.
[5] λίθον ἢ ξύλον PV, ξύλον ἢ λίθον M An.
[6] ὁ ἀββᾶς εἶπεν P, ἀπόκρισις M.
[7] εἰπέ μοι σύ om. P.
[8] εἶπεν om.P.
[9] αὐτὴν om. P.
[10] ἀββᾶς PM. [11] εἶπεν om. P.
[12] προσκύνεις P.
[13] ἂν εἰ P. [14] εἰ εὕρῃς om. M.
[15] αὐτῷ P, ταῦτα An.
[16] προσκυνῶν P.
[17] μὴ γένοιτο VMAn., om. P.
[18] τοσοῦτον add. M, καὶ om. P.
[19] οὐ δὲ M, δὲ οὐ P.
[20] οὐ δὲ PM.
[21] ἐκ τούτου om. PM.

[a] vid. Gen. xlvii. 31 (Heb. xi. 21.)

παλαιουμένας²² καὶ ἀπαλειφομένας καίομεν, καὶ ἄλλας
νέας²³ ποιοῦμεν, πρὸς ὑπόμνησιν μόνην ἀγαθήν.²⁴

2. Ὁ Ἰουδαῖος εἶπε·¹ διὰ τί βλασφημεῖτε λέγοντες²
υἱὸν ἔχει ὁ θεός;
5   ὁ χριστιανός·³ οὐχ ἡμεῖς ἐσμὲν⁴ οἱ λέγοντες τοῦτο,
ἀλλὰ καὶ ἡ γραφὴ ὑμῶν· λέγει γὰρ ᵇ " Κύριος εἶπε πρός
με υἱός μου εἶ σύ, ἐγὼ σήμερον γεγέννηκά σε." ᵃ
ὁ Ἰουδαῖος·⁶ περὶ Σολομῶντος λέγει ὁ ψαλμός.
ὁ χριστιανός·⁷ πόσου μέρους⁸ τοῦ κόσμου ἐκυρί-
10 ευσεν ὁ Σολομῶν;
ὁ Ἰουδαῖος·⁹ οὐδὲ τοῦ ἡμίσεος, οὐδὲ τοῦ τρίτου μέ-
ρους τοῦ κόσμου.¹⁰
ὁ χριστιανός·¹¹ ἄκουσον οὖν ἄρτι¹² νουνεχῶς καὶ
μάθε¹³ ὅτι οὐ περὶ Σολομῶντος, ἀλλὰ περὶ Χριστοῦ¹⁴
15 λέγει ὁ ψαλμός· εἶπε¹⁵ γὰρ ὅτι " Κύριος εἶπε πρός με
υἱός μου εἶ σύ, ἐγὼ σήμερον γεγέννηκά σε· αἴτησαι
παρ' ἐμοῦ¹⁶ καὶ δώσω σοι ἔθνη τὴν κληρονομίαν σου,
καὶ τὴν κατάσχεσίν σου τὰ πέρατα τῆς γῆς· ποιμανεῖς
αὐτοὺς ἐν ῥάβδῳ σιδηρᾷ, ὡς σκεύη κεραμέως συντρίψεις
20 αὐτοὺς καὶ νῦν βασιλεῖς σύνετε." ᵇ ¹⁷ εἰπέ μοι ἄρτι, σὺ
εἰπάς μοι οὐ κατέσχε Σολομῶν τὰ πέρατα τῆς γῆς,¹⁸ πότε
ἐποίμανεν αὐτοὺς ἐν ῥάβδῳ σιδηρᾷ; πότε ὡς σκεύη
κεραμέως συνέτριψεν αὐτοὺς τοὺς ἐχθρούς;¹⁹ οὐδέποτε.²⁰

---

²² παλαιουμένας ἢ PM.
²³ καινουργίας PMAn.
²⁴ μόνον ἀγαθήν P, ἀγαθὴν μόνον An., μόνον ἀγαθὴν τῶν ἁγίων M.   ¹ εἶπε V, εἶπεν M, om. P.
² λέγοντες ὅτι PM.
³ εἶπεν add. M.
⁴ ἐσμὲν μόνοι PM.   ⁵ γὰρ ὅτι PM.
⁶ εἶπεν add. M.   ⁷ εἶπεν add. M.
⁸ καὶ πόσον μέρος PMAn.
⁹ εἶπεν add. M.
¹⁰ οὐδὲ τὸ ἥμισυ, οὐδὲ τὸ τρίτον P, οὐδὲ τὸ ἥμισυ, οὐδὲ τὸ τρίτον τοῦ κόσμου MAn.   ¹¹ εἶπεν add. M.
¹² ἄρτι om. PAn.
¹³ ἀκριβῶς add. M.
¹⁴ τοῦ Χριστοῦ PMAn.
¹⁵ λέγει PMAn.   ¹⁶ ἐμοί P.

¹⁷ καὶ νῦν βασιλεῖς σύνετε om. PAn.
¹⁸ εἰπέ οὖν μοι ἄρτι σύ· πότε κατέσχεν τὰ πέρατα τῆς γῆς ὁ Σολομῶν; P. εἰπέ μοι οὖν σὺ ἄρτι, Ἰουδαῖε, πάντως δῆλον καὶ ὁμωλογούμενόν ἐστιν, ὡς εἴπομεν, ὅτι ἥμισυ τῆς γῆς Σολομῶν οὐ κατέσχεν, οὐδὲ τὸ τρίτον, ἐκτὸς καὶ μόνον τὴν Ἰουδαίαν γῆν· λοιπὸν, πότε κατέσχεν ὁ Σολομῶν τὰ πέρατα τῆς γῆς; An.
¹⁹ πότε συνέτριψε τοὺς ἐχθροὺς αὐτοῦ ὡς σκεύη κεραμέως; P, πότε δὲ ὡς σκεύη κεραμέως συνέτριψε τοὺς ἐχθροὺς αὐτοῖ; An.
²⁰ οὐδέποτε δηλονότι P, πάντως οὐδέποτε An.

ᵃ Psa. ii. 7.   ᵇ Psa. ii. 7-9.

3. Ὁ Ἰουδαῖος· πῶς λέγει¹ "εἶπε Κύριος πρός με αἴτησαι παρ' ἐμοῦ"; καὶ γὰρ εἰ² υἱός ἐστιν, ὡς λέγετε, πῶς λέγει ὁ Θεὸς ὡς πρὸς δοῦλον αἴτησαι παρ' ἐμοῦ; καὶ πάλιν πῶς³ λέγει "ἐγὼ σήμερον γεγέννηκά σε"; ὑμεῖς δὲ λέγετε ὅτι πρὸ τοῦ κόσμου ὅλου ἐγεννήθη.   5
ὁ χριστιανός· περὶ τοῦ εἰπεῖν τὸν πατέρα πρὸς τὸν υἱόν,⁴ "αἴτησαι παρ' ἐμοῦ, καὶ δώσω σοι ἔθνη,"⁵ μὴ σκανδαλίζου· πολλάκις γὰρ λέγει πατὴρ πρὸς τὸν υἱὸν αὐτοῦ⁶ ἀπὸ πολλῆς ἀγάπης, αἴτησαί με ὃ θέλεις καὶ παράσχω σοι⁷· πάλιν⁸ περὶ τοῦ εἰπεῖν,⁹ "ἐγὼ σή- 10
μερον γεγέννηκά σε," περὶ τῆς κατὰ σάρκα γεννήσεως αὐτοῦ λέγει· εὐδοκίᾳ γὰρ πατρὸς ἐτέχθη ἐκ τῆς ἁγίας Θεοτόκου καὶ ἀεὶ παρθένου Μαρίας.¹⁰

4. Ὁ Ἰουδαῖος· εἰ καὶ πείθεις με ὅτι ἐγεννήθη ἐκ Μαρίας, ἀλλ' οὐκ ἔχεις μοι δεῖξαι ὅτι καὶ πρὸ τοῦ κόσ- 15
μου ἐγεννήθη, ὅτι καὶ¹ Θεός ἐστιν ὁ Χριστὸς ὡς λέγεις.²
ὁ χριστιανός· μὴ ὅλα ὁμοῦ ἐρώτα ἀλλὰ ἓν καὶ ἕν· καὶ ἐλπίζω εἰς τοὺς οἰκτιρμοὺς τοῦ Θεοῦ ὅτι ἐκ τῶν γραφῶν ὑμῶν καὶ τῶν προφητῶν ὑμῶν παραστῶ πάντα τὰ περὶ Χριστοῦ ὄντα ἀληθῆ, καὶ περὶ αὐτοῦ ὑπ' 20
αὐτῶν προκηρυχθέντα.³

5. Πλὴν τοῦτο θέλω μαθεῖν ἐξ ὑμῶν·¹ ὁ Δαβὶδ

---

¹ λέγετε ὅτι P.   ² εἰ om. V.
³ πῶς om. P.
⁴ τὸν υἱὸν ὅτι P.
⁵ καὶ δώσω σοι ἔθνη om. P, ἔθνη om. An.
⁶ πολλάκις γὰρ ὁ βασιλεὺς λέγει πρὸς τὸν υἱὸν αὐτοῦ P. πολλὰ γὰρ καὶ βασιλεὺς πρὸς τὸν αὐτοῦ υἱὸν λέγει An.
⁷ εἴ τι θέλεις καὶ παρέχω σοι pro ὃ θέλεις κ.τ.λ. P, καὶ παρέχω σοι εἴ τι θέλεις An.
⁸ καὶ πάλιν PAn.
⁹ εἰπεῖν ὅτι P.
¹⁰ ὅτι δὲ καὶ πρὸ αἰώνων τοῦ πατρὸς ἐγεννήθη, ὁ Σολομῶν, ὡς ἐκ προσώπου αὐτοῦ τοῦ μονογενοῦς υἱοῦ, λέγει "πρὸ τοῦ τὰ ὄρη γενέσθαι, πρὸ τοῦ τὰς πηγὰς προ-

ελθεῖν, πρὸ δὲ πάντων βουνῶν γεννᾷ με"ᵃ. ἐρωτοῦντι οὖν μοι εἰπέ, τίνα πρὸ πάσης τῆς κτίσεως ἐγέννησεν ὁ Θεός; post Μαρίας add. P.
¹ καὶ ὅτι P.
² λέγετε P.
³ ὁ χριστιανός· πάντα παριστήσω ὑμῖν ἐκ τῶν γραφῶν ὑμῶν καὶ τῶν προφητῶν, ὅτι καὶ πρὸ τοῦ κόσμου ἐγεννήθη καὶ ὅτι Θεός ἐστιν ὁ Χριστός, ὡς λέγομεν, καὶ τὰ περὶ τοῦ Χριστοῦ πάντα ἀληθῆ, καὶ τὰ περὶ αὐτοῦ κηρυχθέντα pro ὁ χριστιανός· μὴ ὅλα κ.τ.λ. P ; totum om. An.
¹ πλὴν τοῦτο ἐρωτῶντός μου εἰπέ P. πλὴν πρῶτον θέλω μαθεῖν ἐξ ὑμῶν· An.

ᵃ Prov. viii. 24-25.

βασιλεὺς ὢν καὶ προφήτης καὶ ἅγιος, τίνα κύριον καὶ δεσπότην εἶχεν;
ὁ Ἰουδαῖος· τοῦτο ἐρώτημα² οὐκ ἔχει· ὁ Δαβὶδ γὰρ κύριον ἄλλον³ οὐκ ἔχει, εἰ μὴ τὸν θεον τὸν ποιήσαντα
5 τὸν οὐρανὸν καὶ τὴν γῆν.
ὁ χριστιανός· ὀρθῶς εἶπας. ἰδοὺ οὖν αὐτὸς⁴ λέγει περὶ Χριστοῦ⁵ ὅτι κύριος αὐτοῦ ἐστιν, ὅτι καὶ⁶ πρὸ αἰώνων⁷ ἐγεννήθη· ἐν γὰρ τῷ ἑκατοστῷ ἐννάτῳ⁸ ψαλμῷ λέγει οὕτως, " εἶπεν ὁ κύριος τῷ κυρίῳ μου,
10 κάθου ἐκ δεξιῶν μου·"ᵃ ἰδοὺ οὖν αὐτὸς⁹ τὸν υἱὸν κύριον¹⁰ ὁμολογεῖ· πρὸς αὐτὸν γὰρ εἶπεν¹¹ ὁ πατήρ, μετὰ τὴν ἁγίαν αὐτοῦ σάρκωσιν καὶ ἀνάληψιν, " κάθου ἐκ δεξιῶν μου, ἕως ἂν θῶ τοὺς ἐχθρούς σου ὑποπόδιον τῶν ποδῶν σου·"ᵇ " ἐν ταῖς λαμπρότησι τῶν ἁγίων
15 σου, ἐκ γαστρὸς¹² πρὸ ἑωσφόρου ἐγέννησά σε."ᶜ τίς γὰρ¹³ ἐγεννήθη πρὸ ἑωσφόρου; ἆρα περὶ τοῦ Ἀδὰμ λέγει; οὐδαμῶς· μετὰ δύο γὰρ¹⁴ ἡμέρας τοῦ ἑωσφόρου καὶ τῶν ἀστέρων ἐγένετο. ἀλλ' ἆρα¹⁵ περὶ τοῦ εἰλημμένου¹⁶ ὑμῶν λέγει; ἀλλ'¹⁷ υἱὸν Δαβὶδ¹⁸ λέγει¹⁹ εἶναι·
20 ὁ δὲ Δαβὶδ μετὰ πολλοὺς²⁰ τοῦ Ἀδὰμ ἐγεννήθη· ὁ δὲ Ἀδὰμ τῇ ἕκτῃ ἡμέρᾳ ἐπλάσθη· οἱ δὲ ἑωσφόροι τῇ τετάρτῃ²¹ ἡμέρᾳ ἐγένοντο ὁ δὲ θεὸς λέγει περὶ τοῦ ἰδίου υἱοῦ²² ὅτι " πρὸ ἑωσφόρου ἐγέννησά²³ σε,²⁴ σὺ εἶ²⁵ ἱερεὺς εἰς τὴν αἰῶνα κατὰ τὴν τάξιν Μελχισεδέκ,"²⁶ᵈ τουτέσ-

---

² ἐρώτημα τοῦτο P.
³ αὐτοῦ pro ἄλλον P.
⁴ αὐτὸς ὁ Δαβὶδ PAn.
⁵ τοῦ χριστοῦ PAn.
⁶ καὶ ὅτι P, καὶ ὅτι καὶ An.
⁷ τῶν αἰώνων PAn.   ⁸ ρθ PAn.
⁹ οὖν αὐτός om. P; ἰδοὺ οὖν τὸν υἱὸν τοῦ θεοῦ An.
¹⁰ κύριον ἑαυτοῦ P, κύριον ἑαυτοῦ καλεῖ An.
¹¹ καὶ πρὸς αὐτὸν εἶπεν P.
¹² καὶ ἐκ γαστρὸς P.
¹³ γὰρ om. P.   ¹⁴ γὰρ δύο PAn.
¹⁵ ἆρα om. PAn.
¹⁶ εἰλειμμένου V.
¹⁷ ἀλλὰ PAn.

¹⁸ Δαβὶδ V, τοῦ Δαβὶδ αὐτὸν P, Δαβὶδ αὐτὸν An.
¹⁹ λέγεται P, οὐ λέγεται An.
²⁰ πολλοὺς χρόνους PAn.
²¹ τετάρτῃ VAn., δ´ P.
²² ὁ δὲ θεὸς περὶ τοῦ ἰδίου υἱοῦ λέγει PAn.
²³ ἐγέννησά VAn., γεγέννηκά P.
²⁴ καὶ ὅτι φησὶ post σε add P.
²⁵ εἶ om. PAn.
²⁶ ἐπείδης ἆρα κἂν ἄρτι ὅτι περὶ τοῦ Χριστοῦ καὶ θεοῦ ἡμῶν ἐστιν οὗτος ὁ λόγος; αὐτὸς γάρ ἐστιν ἱερεὺς εἰς τὸν αἰῶνα κατὰ τὴν τάξιν Μελχισεδέκ, post Μελχισεδέκ add. P.

ᵃ Psa. cix. 1.   ᵇ Ibid. vers. 1.   ᶜ Ibid. vers. 3.   ᵈ Ibid. vers. 3-4.

τιν ἱερεὺς τῶν ἐθνῶν· καὶ γὰρ ὁ Μελχισεδὲκ²⁷ ἱερεὺς
ἦν τῶν ἐθνῶν,²⁸ καὶ ἄρτον καὶ οἶνον²⁹ προσέφερεν, ὡς
μαρτυρεῖ πάλιν ἡ γραφὴ ὑμῶν·ᵉ ὅτι ὅτε ἐδέξατο τὸν
Ἀβραὰμ ὁ Μελχισεδὲκ ἐν ἄρτῳ καὶ οἴνῳ ἔθυσε τῷ
θεῷ,³⁰ καθὼς καὶ ὁ Χριστὸς ἀρχιερεὺς παρέδωκεν ἡμῖν,³¹   5
θύειν αὐτῷ ἀναίμακτον θυσίαν κατὰ τὴν τάξιν Μελχισεδέκ. ἄκουσον οὖν πάλιν διὰ Σολομῶντος λέγοντος
τοῦ υἱοῦ³² "πρὸ τοῦ τὰ ὄρη γενέσθαι, πρὸ τοῦ τὰς
πηγὰς προελθεῖν, πρὸ δὲ πάντων τῶν³³ βουνῶν, γεννᾷ
με·"ᶠ δεῖξόν μοι πρὸ πάσης τῆς κτίσεως τίνα ὁ θεὸς   10
ἐγέννησεν.³⁴ ὡσαύτως πάλιν ἐν τῷ ἑβδομηκοστῷ πρώ-
τῳ³⁵ ψαλμῷ λέγει³⁶ "ὁ θεός, τὸ κρίμα σου τῷ βασιλεῖ
δός, καὶ τὴν δικαιοσύνην σου τῷ υἱῷ τοῦ βασιλέως."ᵍ
καὶ ἵνα μὴ³⁷ εἴπῃς ὅτι περὶ Σολομῶντος λέγει,³⁸ εὐθὺς
εἶπε, μετ' ὀλίγους στίχους,³⁹ "καὶ κατακυριεύσει ἀπὸ   15
θαλάσσης ἕως θαλάσσης,"ʰ καὶ "πρὸ τοῦ ἡλίου δι-
αμένει τὸ ὄνομα αὐτοῦ,"ⁱ "καὶ πρὸ τῆς σελήνης γενεὰς
γενεῶν."ᵏ ἰδοὺ ἔδειξά σοι σαφῶς, καὶ διὰ Δαβὶδ καὶ
διὰ Σολομῶντος, ὅτι πρὸ πάσης κτίσεως υἱὸς⁴⁰ ἐκ πα-
τρὸς⁴¹ ὡς οἶδε μόνος αὐτός.   20
6. Πλὴν ἐκεῖνο εἴπατέ μοι¹ ὑμεῖς, καὶ εὐθέως φαίνεται ἡ ἀλήθεια, τὸν εἰλημμένον² ἐκδέχεσθε³ καὶ⁴ τί λέ-

---

²⁷ καὶ γὰρ ὁ Μελχισεδὲκ V. ὁ γὰρ P.
Μελχισεδὲκ PAn.
²⁸ τῶν ἐθνῶν ἦν ἱερεὺς P. om. An.
²⁹ καὶ οἶνον καὶ ἄρτον P. οἶνον
καὶ ἄρτον An.
³⁰ κυρίῳ P.
³¹ ὁ Χριστὸς ἀρχιερεὺς παρέδωκεν
ἡμῖν V. ὁ Χριστὸς ὁ ἀρχιερεὺς ἡμῶν
παρέδωκεν ἡμᾶς An. αὐτὸς ὁ κύριος ἡμῶν ἐνετείλατο ἡμῖν P.
³² καὶ αὐτοῦ δὲ πάλιν ἄκουσον
διὰ Σολομῶντος λέγοντος τοῦ υἱοῦ
ὅτι P. ἄκουσον δὲ καὶ Σολομῶντος
λέγοντος περὶ τῆς πρὸ αἰώνων
γεννήσεως τοῦ μονογενοῦς υἱοῦ
τοῦ θεοῦ An. ³³ τῶν om. PAn.
³⁴ δεῖξόν μοι λοιπὸν τίνα ὁ θεὸς
πρὸ πάσης τῆς κτίσεως ἐγέννησεν

δεῖξόν μοι οὖν τίνα ὁ θεὸς πρὸ
πάσης τῆς κτίσεως ἐγέννησεν An.
ἀλλ' οὐκ ἂν ἔχεις, ὦ Ἰουδαῖε,
τοῦτο ἀπὸ τῶν γραφῶν πιστώσασθαι; add. P.
³⁵ οα' P.
³⁶ λέγει ὁ Δαβὶδ P.
³⁷ ἀναισχυντῶν πάλιν, ὦ Ἰουδαῖε
post μὴ add. P.
³⁸ ταῦτα εἴρηται P.
³⁹ εὐθὺς εἶπε κ.τ.λ. V. ἄκουσον
τί μετ' ὀλίγα εἴρηκεν P.
⁴⁰ ἐγεννήθη ὁ υἱὸς PAn.
⁴¹ τοῦ πατρὸς PAn.
¹ μοι om. P.
² ἠλειμμένον V.
³ ὃν ἐκδέχεσθε PAn.
⁴ καὶ om. PAn.

ᵉ cf. Gen. xiv. 18 sq.   ᶠ Prov. viii. 24-25.   ᵍ Psa. lxxi. 1.
ʰ Ibid. vers. 8.   ⁱ Ibid. 17.   ᵏ Ibid. 5.

56

γετε αυτὸν εἶναι,⁵ Θεὸν σαρκωθέντα, ἢ ἄνθρωπον ψιλὸν ὡς τὸν Δαβὶδ καὶ τοὺς λοιποὺς ἀνθρώπους;
ὁ Ἰουδαῖος· ἄνθρωπον αὐτὸν λέγομεν ὡς ἕνα τῶν προφητῶν καὶ οὐ Θεόν· οὐκ ἔστι γὰρ εἰ μὴ εἷς καὶ μόνος
5 ὁ Θεὸς,⁶ καὶ οὐ δύο ὡς⁷ ὑμεῖς νομίζετε.
7. Τότε ὁ χριστιανὸς διεμαρτύρατο μεγάλῃ τῇ φωνῇ, λέγων τῷ ὄχλῳ,¹ Βλέπετε κύριοι,² τί λέγουσιν ὅτι ἄνθρωπός ἐστι ψιλὸς³ ὁ ἐρχόμενος Χριστὸς αὐτῶν.⁴ ἴδωμεν⁵ οὖν ἄρτι τοὺς προφήτας, καὶ εἰ μὲν⁶ Θεὸν ἐκήρυ-
10 ξαν τὸν ἐρχόμενον χριστὸν, δῆλον ὅτι ὁ ἐλθὼν,⁷ καὶ⁸ παρ' ἡμῶν τῶν χριστιανῶν⁹ πιστευόμενο⁵ ¹⁰ καὶ προσκυνούμενος, αὐτός ἐστιν ἀληθῶς ὁ ὄντως ἀληθὴς ¹¹ Χριστὸς,¹² ὃν δὲ ἐκδέχονται οὗτοι ὅτι ἔρχεται ¹³ πλάνος ἐστι καὶ ἀντίχριστος· εἰ δὲ πάλιν οὐ ¹⁴ παραστήσομεν ¹⁵ τοὺς
15 προφήτας λέγοντας αὐτὸν Θεὸν,¹⁶ δῆλον ὅτι ἡμεῖς ἐσμὲν πλάνοι καὶ Ἰουδαῖοι ἀληθεύουσι.
τότε ἠνέγκασεν ¹⁷ αὐτοὺς καὶ ἤγαγον αὐτοὶ τὰς βίβλους αὐτῶν ἐκ τῆς ἰδίας συναγωγῆς, ἵνα ¹⁸ ἐξ αὐτῶν ἐλεγχθῶσι.¹⁹
20 8. Καὶ προλαβὼν ἐρωτᾷ αὐτοὺς καὶ λέγει " εὐλογημένος ὁ ἐρχόμενος." ᵃ ¹ τίς οὗτός ἐστιν ² ὁ ἐρχόμενος;
ὁ Ἰουδαῖος·³ ὁ Χριστὸς ὁ υἱὸς τοῦ Δαβίδ.
ὁ χριστιανός· " εὐλογημένος ὁ ἐρχόμενος ἐν ὀνόματι κυρίου· Θεὸς κύριος καὶ ἐπέφανεν ἡμῖν." ᵇ ἤρξαντο οὖν
25 κράζειν οἱ Ἰουδαῖοι, " ἐπιφάνηθι ἡμῖν" λέγει, μέλλοντα

⁵ εἶναι αὐτόν P. εἶναι om. An.
⁶ ὁ Θεὸς VAn., ὁ om. P.
⁷ ὡς καθὼς P. καθάπερ An.
¹ τῇ φωνῇ, παντὶ τῷ ὄχλῳ λέγων P.
² βλέπετε καὶ ἀκούετε, ὦ κύριοι P.
³ ψιλός ἐστιν P.
⁴ αὐτῶν Χριστός P.
⁵ ἐνέγκωμεν PAn.
⁶ μὲν om. PAn.
⁷ Χριστὸς καὶ Θεὸς ἡμῶν ὁ λατρευόμενος post ἐλθὼν add. P.
⁸ καὶ om. P.
⁹ τῶν χριστιανῶν om. P.

¹⁰ καὶ πιστευόμενος P.
¹¹ ὁ ὄντως ἀληθὴς om. P.
¹² Θεὸς καὶ Χριστὸς P.
¹³ ὅτι ἔρχεται om. An. καὶ λέγουσιν ἔρχεσθαι P.
¹⁴ πάλιν οὐ V. μὴ P. πάλιν μὴ An.
¹⁵ παραστήσωμεν PAn.
¹⁶ Θεὸν PAn. Χριστὸν V.
¹⁷ ἠνάγκασεν (sic) V.
¹⁸ ὅπως P.
¹⁹ διαλεχθῶσιν P.
¹ " εὐλογημένος ὁ ἐρχόμενος ἐν ὀνόματι κυρίου" P.
² ἐστιν οὗτος P.
³ οἱ Ἰουδαῖοι P.

ᵃ Psa. cxvii. 26.   ᵇ Ib. vers. 26, 27.

γὰρ δηλοῖ χρόνον. κατασείσας δὲ αὐτοὺς ὁ χριστιανὸς
τῇ χειρὶ εἶπε, καλῶς λέγετε, μελλητικόν ἐστιν· τέως τὸν
ἐρχόμενον Θεὸν καὶ κύριον λέγει, εἰπὼν "Θεὸς κύριος
καὶ ἐπέφανεν ἡμῖν." εἴτε οὖν ἐπέφανεν, εἴτε ἐπιφάναι
μέλλει, οὐκ ἔστιν ὁ Χριστὸς ὑμῶν, ἀλλ' ἡμέτερος· ὑμεῖς   5
γὰρ ἄνθρωπον ἐκδέχεσθε τὸν ἐρχόμενον, ἀλλ' οὐ Θεόν.
ὁ δὲ Δαβὶδ κύριον καὶ Θεὸν τὸν ἐλθόντα καὶ ἐρχόμενον ἐκήρυξεν· ὁμοίως καὶ ὁ Ἀββακοὺμ καὶ Ἡσαΐας
καὶ πάντες οἱ προφῆται Θεὸν τὸν ἐρχόμενον ἐκήρυξαν·
Ἡσαΐας μὲν ἔλεγεν ὅτι "παιδίον ἐγεννήθη ἡμῖν, υἱὸς   10
καὶ ἐδόθη ἡμῖν· καὶ καλεῖται τὸ ὄνομα αὐτοῦ μεγάλης
βουλῆς ἄγγελος, θαυμαστὸς σύμβουλος, Θεὸς ἰσχυρός,
ἐξουσιαστής, ἄρχων εἰρήνης, πατὴρ τοῦ μέλλοντος αἰῶνος." ὡσαύτως καὶ ὁ Ἀββακοὺμ φησὶν "ὁ Θεὸς
ἀπὸ Θαιμὰν ἥξει." καὶ Ἱερεμίας δὲ φησὶν "οὗτος   15
ὁ Θεὸς ἡμῶν, οὐ λογισθήσεται ἕτερος πρὸς αὐτόν· ἐξευ-
ρὼν πᾶσαν ὁδὸν ἐπιστήμης ἔδωκεν αὐτὴν Ἰακὼβ τῷ
παιδὶ αὐτοῦ, καὶ Ἰσραὴλ τῷ ἠγαπημένῳ ὑπ' αὐτοῦ.
μετὰ ταῦτα ἐπὶ γῆς ὤφθη, καὶ τοῖς ἀνθρώποις συναν-
εστράφη." βλέπεις ὅτι Θεὸν ἀληθινὸν ἐκήρυξαν   20
τὸν ἐπὶ γῆς ὀφθέντα καὶ τοῖς ἀνθρώποις συναναστρα-
φέντα.

---

⁴ μέλλοντα γὰρ κ.τ.λ. V. μελλητικόν ἐστιν P.
⁵ τῇ χειρὶ ὁ χριστιανὸς P.
⁶ Θεὸν καὶ κύριον τὸν ἐρχόμενον P.
⁷ ἐπιφανῆναι An.
⁸ εἴτε οὖν ἐπέφανεν κ.τ.λ. VAn.
εἴτε δὲ ἐπιφάναι μέλλει, εἴτε ἐπέφανεν P.
⁹ ὁ ἡμέτερος P.
¹⁰ ὑμεῖς γὰρ ἄνθρωπον ψιλὸν
τὸν ἐρχόμενον ἐκδέχεσθε, καὶ οὐ
Θεόν P. ὑμεῖς γὰρ ἄνθρωπον τὸν
ἐρχόμενον ἐκδέχεσθε, καὶ οὐ Θεόν
An.   ¹¹ Θεὸν καὶ κύριον PAn.
¹² ὁ om. P.   ¹³ Ἀμβακοὺμ P.
¹⁴ Ἱερεμίας καὶ Μαλαχίας add.
P. ὁμοίως κ.τ.λ. ..... ἐκήρυξαν
om. An.

¹⁵ τὸν ἐρχόμενον Θεόν P.
¹⁶ λέγων P. λέγει An.
¹⁷ ποῖος οὖν ἄνθρωπος, καθὼς
ὑμεῖς λέγετε, ψιλός ἐστι Θεὸς ἰσχυρός, ἐξουσιαστής, πατὴρ τοῦ μέλλοντος αἰῶνος; post αἰῶνος add.
P. ποῖος ἄνθρωπος, καθὼς ὑμεῖς
λέγετε, δύναται εἶναι Θεὸς ἰσχυρός, ἐξουσιαστής, ἄρχων εἰρήνης,
πατὴρ τοῦ μέλλοντος αἰῶνος; add.
An.
¹⁸ Ἀμβακοὺμ ὁ προφήτης P.
¹⁹ Θεμὰν P.
²⁰ δὲ πάλιν P.
²¹ ἐξεῦρεν PAn.
²² καὶ ἔδωκεν PAn.
²³ ἐπὶ γῆς VAn., ἐπὶ τῆς γῆς P.
²⁴ ὁρᾷς P.
²⁵ ἀληθῆ P.

ᵉ Psa. cxvii. 26.   ᵈ Isa. ix. 6.   ᵉ Hab. iii. 3.   ᶠ Baruch iii. 36-38.

9. Καὶ πάλιν ὁ Δαβὶδ λέγει περὶ αὐτοῦ ὅτι¹ "ἐβασίλευσεν ὁ θεὸς ἐπὶ πάντα² τὰ ἔθνη"·ᵃ διὰ τί οὐκ εἶπεν³ ἐβασίλευσεν ὁ θεὸς ἐπὶ τοὺς Ἰουδαίους; καὶ πάλιν ὅτι "ἴδωσαν⁴ πάντα τὰ ἔθνη τὸ σωτήριον τοῦ θεοῦ ἡμῶν·"ᵇ καὶ πάλιν "πάντα τὰ ἔθνη κροτήσατε χεῖρας"·ᶜ καὶ πάλιν "εἴπατε ἐν τοῖς ἔθνεσιν ὅτι κύριος ἐβασίλευσεν."ᵈ⁵ καὶ Ἠσαΐας πάλιν περὶ ὑμῶν, μᾶλλον δὲ δι' αὐτοῦ ὁ θεὸς εἶπεν,ᵉ ὅτι "καλέσω τὸν οὐ λαόν μου λαόν μου, καὶ τὸν ἠλεημένον οὐκ ἠλεημένον,"ᵉ⁷ τουτέστι τὴν συναγωγὴν ὑμῶν.⁸ ὡσαύτως καὶ Ἰακὼβ ὁ πατριάρχης, προφητεύων περὶ Χριστοῦ,⁹ εὐλογῶν τὸν Ἰούδαν, εἶπεν¹⁰ "οὐκ ἐκλείψει ἄρχων ἐξ Ἰούδα οὐδὲ¹¹ ἡγούμενος ἐκ τῶν μηρῶν αὐτοῦ ἕως ἂν ἔλθῃ ᾧ¹² ἀπόκειται καὶ αὐτὸς προσδοκία ἐθνῶν."ᶠ προσέχετε, ἄνδρες,¹³ τί Ἰακὼβ εἶπεν "οὐκ ἐκλείψει ἄρχων ἐξ Ἰούδα οὐδὲ¹⁴ ἡγούμενος ἐκ τῶν μηρῶν αὐτοῦ ἕως ἂν ἔλθῃ ᾧ¹⁵ ἀπόκειται," τουτέστιν ὁ χριστός, "καὶ αὐτὸς προσδοκία ἐθνῶν."¹⁶ ὡς εἰς¹⁷ μάτην προσδοκῶσιν¹⁸ Ἰουδαῖοι ὃν προσδοκῶσιν· ¹⁹ ὃν γὰρ προσεδοκοῦμεν τὰ ἔθνη Χρισ-

¹ λέγει περὶ αὐτοῦ An., περὶ αὐτοῦ λέγει P, λέγει περὶ ἑαυτοῦ ὅτι V.
² πάντα om. PAn.
³ εἶπεν ὅτι PAn.   ⁴ εἴδωσαν P.
⁵ καὶ πάλιν ὁ Δαβὶδ "πάντα τὰ ἔθνη ὅσα ἐποίησας ἥξουσιν καὶ προσκυνήσουσιν ἐνώπιόν σου, κύριε. καὶ δοξάσουσι τὸ ὄνομά σου ὅτι μέγας εἶ σύ, καὶ ποίων θαυμάσια σὺ εἶ ὁ θεὸς μόνος."ᵍ καὶ Μαλαχίας δὲ περὶ τῶν ἐθνῶν διαρρήδην φάσκει, λέγων "οὐκ ἔστιν μου θέλημα ἐν ὑμῖν," τουτέστιν ἐν τοῖς Ἰουδαίοις, "διότι ἀπὸ ἀνατολῶν ἡλίου καὶ ἕως δυσμῶν τὸ ὄνομά μου δεδόξασται ἐν τοῖς ἔθνεσιν"ʰ post ἐβασίλευσεν add. P.
⁶ καὶ Ἠσαΐας πάλιν περὶ ὑμῶν, κ.τ.λ. V, καὶ πάλιν διὰ τοῦ Ὡσηὲ τοῦ προφήτου λέγει P, καὶ πάλιν Ὡσηέ. An.

⁷ καὶ τὸν ἠλεημένον κ.τ.λ. V, καὶ τὴν οὐκ ἠγαπημένην ἠγαπημένην P, καὶ τὴν ἠλεημένην οὐκ ἠλεημένην An.
⁸ τὴν συναγωγὴν ὑμῶν V, τὴν ἐκκλησίαν P, τὴν συναγωγὴν τῶν Ἰουδαίων An.
⁹ τοῦ χριστοῦ καὶ P.
¹⁰ εἶπεν om. et ἐξ οὗ ἔμελλεν Χριστὸς τὸ κατὰ σάρκα παραγίνεσθαι, οὕτω πῶς φησὶ post Ἰούδαν add. P.
¹¹ οὐδὲ VAn., καὶ P.
¹² ᾧ PAn., ὃ V.
¹³ ὦ ἄνδρες P.   ¹⁴ καὶ P.
¹⁵ ᾧ PAn., ὃ V.
¹⁶ οὐκ εἶπεν τὸν ἐρχόμενον ἔσεσθαι προσδοκίαν Ἰουδαίων, ἀλλὰ προσδοκίαν ἐθνῶν post ἐθνῶν add. P.
¹⁷ ὥστε PAn.
¹⁸ προσδοκοῦσιν P.
¹⁹ προσκυνοῦσι P.

ᵃ Psa. xlvi. 9.   ᵇ Psa. xcvii. 5.   ᶜ Psa. xlvi. 1.   ᵈ Psa. xcv. 10.
ᵉ Hos. ii, 23.   ᶠ Gen. xlix. 10.   ᵍ Psa. lxxxv. 9-10.   ʰ Mal. i. 10-11.

τὸν, ἰδοὺ ἦλθεν· ²⁰ διὰ τοῦτο²¹ ἐξέλιπεν ἄρχων ἐξ Ἰούδα καὶ ἡγούμενος καὶ ²² πάντα τὰ ἀγαθά.

ἐπεὶ δεῖξόν²³ μοι²⁴ ἀφ' οὗ ἐσταυρώθη ὁ χριστός; ποῖος προφήτης εὑρέθη ἐν²⁵ ὑμῖν; ποῖον βασίλειον²⁶ ἔχετε σήμερον; ποῦ εἰσὶν οἱ κριταὶ ὑμῶν; ποῦ οἱ ἄρχοντες; ἐξέλιπον.²⁷ ποῦ αἱ θυσίαι ὑμῶν; ποῦ ὁ ναὸς ὑμῶν;²⁸ ἰδοὺ κεῖται ἔρημος κατὰ τὸν λόγον τοῦ χριστοῦ²⁹ ἡμῶν, τοῦ εἰπόντος οὐ μὴ μείνῃ λίθος εἰς αὐτὸν³⁰ ἐπὶ λίθον.³¹ ¹ ἆρα μὴ³² οὐκ ἐγένετο ὁ λόγος τοῦ χριστοῦ; εἶπεν³³ "ἐλεύσονται καὶ ἀροῦσι Ῥωμαῖοι τὴν βασιλείαν ἀφ' ὑμῶν·"³⁴ ᵏ καὶ ἰδοὺ ἐπήρθη³⁵ ἡ βασιλεία ἐξ ὑμῶν καὶ ἡ προφητεία καὶ ἡ λατρεία καὶ ἡ θυσία. ποῦ εἰσὶν αἱ πλάκες³⁶ ἃς ἐλάβετε; ἰδοὺ ἀπώλοντο. ποῦ ἡ κιβωτὸς ὑμῶν τῆς διαθήκης;³⁷ ἰδοὺ οὐ φαίνεται. ποῦ τὸ θυσιαστήριον ὁ ἐποίησε Μωυσῆς; ποῦ ἡ ῥάβδος ἡ³⁸ βλαστήσασα; ποῦ ἡ στάμνος καὶ τὸ μάννα; ποῦ ἡ ἐπισκίασις τοῦ ναοῦ καὶ ὁ καθαρισμὸς τοῦ αἵματος; ποῦ τὸ πῦρ τὸ κατερχόμενον ἐκ τοῦ οὐρανοῦ; ποῦ παρ' ὑμῶν³⁹ εἷς ἀντὶ Μωυσέως; ποῦ⁴⁰ ἕνα προφήτην εὑρίσκετε; ποῦ ἡ ὀρτυγομήτρα καὶ τὸ μάννα; οὐδὲν ἀληθῶς ἔχετε, οὐδέν· κατὰ τὴν τῶν τριῶν παίδων φωνὴν⁴¹ τὴν λέγουσαν⁴² "οὐκ ἔστιν ἐν τῷ καιρῷ τούτῳ ἄρχων καὶ προφήτης καὶ ἡγούμενος· οὐδὲ ὁλοκαύτωσις, οὐδὲ θυσία, οὐδὲ

---

²⁰ ὃν γὰρ τὰ ἔθνη προσδοκοῦσι Χριστὸν, ἦλθε· An., ἰδοὺ γὰρ ὃν προσδοκοῦμεν τὰ ἔθνη, ἦλθεν· P.
²¹ διὰ τοῦτο καὶ An., ἐκ τούτου οὖν δῆλον ὅτι P.
²² οὐ μὴν ἀλλὰ καὶ P.
²³ ἐπεὶ, δεῖξόν V, ἐπίδειξόν P.
²⁴ μοι λοιπὸν, ὦ Ἰουδαῖε P.
²⁵ παρ' P.
²⁶ βασιλέα P.
²⁷ οὐκ ἐξέλιπον καθὼς ἡ προφητεία λέγει; P.
²⁸ ὑμῶν om. P.
²⁹ τοῦ χριστοῦ καὶ θεοῦ P.
³⁰ εἰς αὐτὸν PAn. om.
³¹ ἐπὶ λίθον ὧδε P, ἐπὶ λίθον ἐπ' αὐτόν An.
³² μὴ om. P.

³³ εἶπεν ὅτι PAn.
³⁴ οἱ Ῥωμαῖοι καὶ ἀροῦσιν ἀφ' ὑμῶν τὴν βασιλείαν P, οἱ Ῥωμαῖοι καὶ ἀροῦσιν ὑμῶν τὸ ἔθνος, καὶ τὴν πόλιν καὶ τὸ βασίλειον An.
³⁵ ἤρθη P, καὶ ἰδοὺ κ.τ.λ. ...... θυσία om. An.
³⁶ πλάκαι P.
³⁷ τῆς διαθήκης ὑμῶν P. ὑμῶν om. An.
³⁸ ἡ PAn., οὐ V.
³⁹ ὑμῖν P. ποῦ παρ' κ.τ.λ. ..... Μωυσέως; om. An.
⁴⁰ ποῦ κἂν P.
⁴¹ τὴν φωνὴν τῶν τριῶν παίδων PAn.
⁴² τὴν περὶ ὑμῶν λέγουσαν P, τὴν ὑπὲρ ὑμῶν λέγουσαν An.

¹ Cf. Matt. xxiv. 2.   ᵏ John xi. 48.

προσφορὰ, οὐδὲ θυμίαμα, οὐ τόπος τοῦ καταπῶσαι⁴³ ἐνώπιον τοῦ θεοῦ," καὶ εὑρεῖν ἔλεος."¹ ποῖον γὰρ τόπον ἐξ ὧν ὑμῖν ἔδωκεν⁴⁵ ὁ θεὸς ἔχετε σήμερον; ἀλλὰ πάντα ταῦτα ἀφείλετο⁴⁶ ἐξ ὑμῶν δέδωκε καὶ ἡμῖν αὐτά.⁴⁷

5 κἂν τὸ Σινᾶ εἴπῃς ὄρος⁴⁸ ὅπου τὸν νόμον ἐδέξω καὶ οὐ κατεδέξω, ἀλλὰ Χριστὸς ἐκεῖ δοξάζεται σήμερον· ⁴⁹ κἂν τὸν Ἰορδάνην ὅπου⁵⁰ ἐπέρασας εἴπῃς, ἀλλὰ Χριστοῦ ἐκεῖ βαπτισθέντος αὐτὸς παρ' ἡμῖν ἐκεῖ δοξάζεται· κἂν τὴν Ἱερουσαλὴμ καὶ τὴν Σιών σου τὴν παλαιὰν⁵¹ εἴπῃς,
10 ἀλλὰ Χριστοῦ ἐκεῖ σταυρωθέντος τὰ αὐτοῦ παθήματα ἐκεῖ προσκυνοῦνται⁵² σήμερον· κἂν⁵³ τὸ ὄρος τῶν ἐλαιῶν εἴπῃς, καὶ τὴν κοιλάδα τοῦ Ἰωσαφὰτ,⁵⁴ ἀλλὰ Χριστοῦ ἐκεῖθεν ἀναληφθέντος⁵⁵ αὐτὸς κἀκεῖ μεγαλύνεται· κἂν Βηθλεὲμ τὴν πόλιν Δαβὶδ⁵⁶ ζητήσῃς,⁵⁷ ἀλλὰ
15 Χριστοῦ ἐκεῖ τεχθέντος ὡς ἐν οὐρανῷ ἐκεῖ⁵⁸ δοξάζεται πάντοτε· καὶ τί λέγω τὴν Σιών, καὶ Βηθλεὲμ, καὶ τὸν Ἰορδάνην;⁵⁹ πάρελθε δύσιν, ἐπισκόπησον ἀνατολὴν, ἐκζήτησον τὴν ὑπ' οὐρανὸν ὅλην,⁶⁰ αὐτὰς τὰς Βρεττανικὰς νήσους, αὐτὰ τὰ ἑσπέρια καὶ ἔσχατα τοῦ κόσμου,
20 καὶ⁶¹ εὑρήσεις τὰ μὲν Ἰουδαίων καὶ Ἑλλήνων σιωπώμενα, τὰ δὲ Χριστοῦ παντὶ⁶² κηρυττόμενα καὶ τιμώμενα⁶³ καὶ πιστευόμενα καὶ βεβαιούμενα. καὶ μή μοι εἴπῃς ὅτι ἰδοὺ σήμερον καταπονούμεθα οἱ χριστιανοὶ καὶ αἰχμαλωτιζόμεθα, τοῦτο γάρ ἐστι τὸ μέγα,⁶⁴ ὅτι ὑπὸ

⁴³ καὶ ἡγούμενος κ.τ.λ. . . . . καταπῶσαι om. P. οὐδὲ ὁλοκαύτωσις κ.τ.λ. . . . καταπῶσαι om. An. καὶ τὰ ἑξῆς add. PAn.
⁴⁴ οὐκ ἔστιν τόπος add P.
⁴⁵ ἔδωκεν ὑμῖν PAn.
⁴⁶ ἀφείλετο V, ἐπῆρεν An., ἦρεν P.
⁴⁷ καὶ ἡμῖν αὐτὰ ἔδωκεν P. καὶ ἡμῖν αὐτοὺς ἔδωκεν An.
⁴⁸ ὄρος εἴπῃς P. ὄρος om. An.
⁴⁹ ἀλλὰ κἀκεῖ σήμερον Χριστὸς δοξάζεται P.
⁵⁰ ὅπου VAn. ὂν P.
⁵¹ Σιὼν τὴν παλαιάν σου P.
⁵² προσκυνεῖται P.
⁵³ εἰ καὶ P, εἴτε An.
⁵⁴ εἴπῃς post Ἰωσαφὰτ add. P.
⁵⁵ ἐκεῖθεν ἀναληφθέντος Χριστοῦ P.
⁵⁶ τὴν Βηθλεὲμ πόλιν Δαβὶδ An., τὴν πόλιν Δαβὶδ Βηθλεὲμ P.
⁵⁷ ζητήσεις P, εἴπῃς An.
⁵⁸ κἀκεῖ PAn.
⁵⁹ Βηθλεὲμ, καὶ τὴν Σιὼν, καὶ τὸν Ἰορδάνην; P, Βηθλεὲμ, καὶ Σιὼν, καὶ Ἰορδάνην; An.
⁶⁰ ὅλην om. An. πάρελθε δύσιν, ἐπισκόπησον ἀνατολήν post ὅλην add. V. ⁶¹ καὶ ἐκεῖ P.
⁶² πάντα PAn.
⁶³ καὶ τιμώμενα om. P.
⁶⁴ θαυμαστὸν P.

¹ "Hymn of the Three Children," vers. 14.

τοσούτων ἐθνῶν διωκόμενοι καὶ μισούμενοι καὶ πολεμούμενοι, τὴν πίστιν⁶⁵ ἡμῶν ἑστῶσαν⁶⁶ ἔχομεν⁶⁷ καὶ οὐ σβέννυται,⁶⁸ καὶ οὔτε⁶⁹ τὸ βασίλειον ἡμῶν κατήργηται οὔτε⁷⁰ αἱ ἐκκλησίαι ἡμῶν κλείονται, ἀλλὰ καὶ⁷¹ ἀναμέσον τῶν ἐθνῶν τῶν διωκόντων⁷² ἡμᾶς⁷³ ἐκκλησίας 5 ἔχομεν, σταυροὺς⁷⁴ πήσσομεν,⁷⁵ θυσιαστήρια⁷⁶ οἰκοδομοῦμεν, ἐπιτελοῦμεν θυσίας.⁷⁷ ἆρα⁷⁸ τοιούτως⁷⁹ ἄδικός ἐστιν ὁ θεός,⁸⁰ ὡς⁸¹ εἰ ἐγίνωσκεν ὅτι πλανώμεθα οἱ χριστιανοὶ συνεχώρει⁸² ἡμᾶς⁸³ πλανᾶσθαι ἀπόλλυσθαι⁸⁴ τῇ πλάνῃ τούτων γένος ἀνθρώπων;⁸⁵ μὴ γένοιτο. καί- 10 τοι γε οὐκ ἐπαύσατο πάντοτε⁸⁶ πολεμουμένη ἡ πίστις ἡμῶν καὶ ἱσταμένη καὶ⁸⁷ μὴ ἐξαλειφομένη.⁸⁸

10. Εἰ ἄρα κακὴ ἦν πῶς οὐ συνεχώρησεν ὁ θεὸς¹ σβεσθῆναι ἀπὸ τοσούτων Ἑλλήνων, ἀπὸ Περσῶν, ἀπὸ Σαρακηνῶν;² μὴ γάρ μοι εἴπητε ὅτι παιδευόμεθα οἱ χρισ- 15 τιανοί.³ ἀλλ' ἐκεῖνό μοι ἐρευνήσατε⁴ πῶς ἡμῖν τοῖς πλανωμένοις, ὡς λέγετε, τὴν βασιλείαν πάσης τῆς γῆς ὁ θεὸς⁵ ἐπίστευσε; πῶς τὴν τοῦ χριστοῦ⁶ σφραγίδα μέχρι καὶ νῦν οὐδεὶς κατήργησεν⁷ ἢ ἐπᾶραι ἐξ ἡμῶν ἴσχυσε;

---

⁶⁵ ἡ πίστις PAn.
⁶⁶ ἵσταται PAn.
⁶⁷ ἔχομεν om. PAn.
⁶⁸ παύεται PAn.
⁶⁹ καὶ οὔτε V, οὐδὲ PAn.
⁷⁰ οὐδὲ PAn.
⁷¹ καὶ om. PAn.
⁷² τῶν κρατούντων καὶ διωκόντων PAn.
⁷³ ἡμᾶς καὶ P.
⁷⁴ καὶ σταυροὺς PAn.
⁷⁵ πηγνύομεν P.
⁷⁶ καὶ θυσιαστήρια P, καὶ ἐκκλησίας An.
⁷⁷ καὶ θυσίας ἐπιτελοῦμεν P, θυσίας ἐπιτελοῦμεν An.
⁷⁸ ἆρα οὖν P.
⁷⁹ τοιοῦτος PAn.
⁸⁰ ὁ θεός ἐστιν P. ἐστιν om. An.
⁸¹ ὅτι l'An.
⁸² ἤφιεν PAn.
⁸³ οὕτως add. An.
⁸⁴ πλανᾶσθαι ἀπόλλυσθαι V, πλανᾶσθαι ἰδοὺ λοιπὸν χιλίους χρόνους ἀπολέσθαι P, ἰδοὺ λοιπὸν πόσοι χρόνοι ἀπὸ Χριστοῦ ἀπολέσθαι τῇ πλάνῃ An.
⁸⁵ τῇ πλάνῃ τοσοῦτον γένος καὶ πλῆθος ἀνθρώπων PAn.
⁸⁶ πάντοτε οὐκ ἐπαύσατο P.
⁸⁷ μᾶλλον καὶ P.
⁸⁸ μὴ γένοιτο. καίτοι κ.τ.λ. . . . . . ἐξαλειφομένη om. An.
¹ αὐτὴν ὁ θεός P.
² ἀπὸ Σκλαβῶν add. P.
³ μὴ γάρ κ.τ.λ. . . . . . χριστιανοί V, μὴ γάρ μοι τοῦτο σκοπήσητε ἢ εἴπητε ὅτι ἄρτι εἰς τὰ κ' ταῦτα ἔτη παιδευόμεθα οἱ χριστιανοί P, μὴ γὰρ τοῦτο σκοπήσηται ἢ εἴπηται ὅτι ἄρτι εἰς τοσαῦτα ἔτη παιδευόμεθα ἀπὸ τῶν Ἰσραηλιτῶν ἐθνῶν An.
⁴ ἑρμηνεύσατε P, ἑρμηνεῦσαι An.
⁵ ὁ θεός om. P.
⁶ χρυσίου An.
⁷ καταργῆσαι PAn.

πόσοι βασιλεῖς ἐθνῶν, Περσῶν,[8] Ἀρράβων[9] τοῦτο ἐδοκίμασαν καὶ οὐδαμῶς ἴσχυσαν; ἵνα δείξῃ ὁ θεὸς ὅτι κἂν διωκώμεθα οἱ χριστιανοὶ, ἀλλ' ἡμεῖς πάντων βασιλεύομεν, ἡμεῖς πάντων[10] κυριεύομεν· τὸ γὰρ μεθ'[11] ἡμῶν καὶ ἐκ τῆς βασιλείας ἡμῶν σημεῖον τοῦ χριστοῦ ἔστι σήμερον.[11] ἐπεὶ εἰπέ μοι εἰ μὴ σημεῖον ὥς[12] αἰώνιος[13] καὶ[14] ἀνίκητος καὶ ἀνεξάλειπτος ἡ πίστις[15] τῶν χριστιανῶν καὶ ἡ βασιλεία,[16] πῶς τὸν σταυρὸν[17] πάντες ὑμεῖς καὶ οἱ ἐχθροὶ[18] ἡμῶν μισεῖτε[19] καὶ βλασφημεῖτε;[20] ἀλλὰ καὶ ἂν[21] χρυσοῦν[22] σταυρὸν[23] ἴδητε, βδελύσσεσθε[24] καὶ ἀποστρέφεσθε. ὄντως καλῶς περὶ ὑμῶν ὁ Δαβὶδ[25] εἶπεν[26] "ὀφθαλμοὺς ἔχουσι καὶ οὐκ ὄψονται, καρδίαν[27] ἔχουσι καὶ οὐ συνήσουσιν."[28] [a] πῶς ὅπερ πολεμεῖτε τοῦτο ποθεῖτε, καὶ ὅπερ βδελύσσεσθε[29] τοῦτο προθύμως καταδέχεσθε παραδόξως νικώμενοι; καὶ[30] εἰ ἄρα[31] φρόνησιν εἴχετε[32] ἤρκει καὶ ὑμῖν[33] πᾶσι[34] τοῦτο τὸ σημεῖον[35] καὶ τὸ πρᾶγμα εἰς τὸ πεῖσαι καὶ δεῖξαι[36] ὅτι[37] ὁ σταυρὸς τοῦ χριστοῦ εἰς τοὺς[38] αἰῶνας πανταχοῦ[39] βασιλεύει, πανταχοῦ[40] πολιτεύεται. πόσοι τὴν πίστιν ἡμῶν καὶ

[8] Ἰουδαίων add. P.
[9] Ἀρράβων PAn., Ἀράβων V.
[10] βασιλεύομεν, ἡμεῖς πάντων om. P. ἡμεῖς πάντων κυριεύομεν om. An.
[11] τὸ γὰρ μεθ' κ.τ.λ. PV, τὸ γὰρ σημεῖον τοῦ χρυσίου τῆς βασιλείας ἡμῶν, σημεῖον τοῦ χριστοῦ αὐτοῦ ἐστὶν· An.
[12] ἐστιν P, ἣν ὅτι An.
[13] αἰώνιον P. [14] ἡ P.
[15] ἡ πίστις V, πιστις P, ἣν ἡ πίστις An.
[16] καὶ βασιλεία τῶν χριστιανῶν; P.
[17] τοῦ χριστοῦ add. PAn.
[18] οἱ λοιποὶ ἐχθροὶ P, καὶ οἱ ἐχθροὶ om. An.
[19] μισοῦντες PAn.
[20] βλασφημοῦντες, ἀποστρέψαι οὐ δύνασθε, ἀλλὰ τοῦτον προθύμως καταδέχεσθε; P, βλασφημοῦντες, ἐκπεπτώκατε; πῶς τὸν σταυρὸν ἐκ τοῦ χρυσίου ἀπαλεῖψαι οὐ

δύνασθε, ἀλλὰ καὶ τοῦτον προθύμως δέχεσθε; An.
[21] ἐὰν PAn. [22] χρυσὸν P.
[23] βδελύσσεσθε P.
[24] χωρὶς σταυροῦ An.
[25] ὁ Δαβὶδ περὶ ὑμῶν P.
[26] καὶ ὁ Ἡσαΐας add. P.
[27] καὶ καρδίαν P.
[28] συνιοῦσι PAn.
[29] βδελύττεσθε P. [30] καί om. P.
[31] ἄρα οὖν P, ἄρα νοῦν An.
[32] καὶ νοῦν add. P.
[33] ὑμῖν καὶ pro καὶ ὑμῖν PAn.
[34] τοῖς ἀπίστοις add. P.
[35] τὸ σημεῖον τοῦτο P.
[36] πεῖσαι καὶ δεῖξαι V, δεῖξαι καὶ πεῖσαι PAn.
[37] ἡ πίστις καὶ add. PAn.
[38] τοὺς om. PAn.
[39] πάντας P, πάντοτε An.
[40] πανταχοῦ V, καὶ παντὶ τῷ κόσμῳ P, πανταχοῦ πολιτεύεται om. An.

[a] Jer. v. 21.

τὴν ἐκκλησίαν κλεῖσαι καὶ καταργῆσαι ἐδοκίμασαν καὶ οὐκ ἴσχυσαν; ἀλλ' αὐτοὶ μὲν παρῆλθον, ὁ δὲ "θεμέλιος"⁴¹ ἡμῶν καὶ ἡ πίστις⁴² ἵσταται ἀσάλευτος"ᵇ διὰ τὸν⁴³ Χριστὸν τὸν" εἰπόντα⁴⁵ ὅτι "πύλαι ᾅδου οὐ κατισχύσουσιν αὐτῆς."ᶜ ποῦ ἔστι Διοκλητιανὸς,⁴⁶ καὶ⁴⁷ 5 Μαξιμιανός;⁴⁸ ποῦ ἔστιν⁴⁹ Ἡρώδης; ποῦ ἔστιν Ὀυεσπασιανὸς,⁵⁰ καὶ πάντες οἱ τοῦ Χριστοῦ τοὺς⁵¹ μάρτυρας ἀποκτείναντες; τὴν δὲ πίστιν ἡμῶν μὴ παύσαντες μηδὲ κλείσαντες,⁵² καὶ αὐτοὶ μὲν ἀπώλοντο, ὁ δὲ Χριστὸς⁵³ οὐκ ἐψεύσατο⁵⁴ εἰπὼν "ἔσεσθε μισούμενοι ὑπὸ πάντων 10 διὰ τὸ ὄνομά μου·"⁵⁵ᵈ ἐν οὖν ἐκ τῶν δύο ἐπιλέξασθε, ἢ μὴ μισῆτε⁵⁶ ἡμᾶς, μήτε⁵⁷ ὑμεῖς μήτε⁵⁸ τὰ ἔθνη, ἢ ἐὰν μισῆτε⁵⁹ ἡμᾶς, πάντως⁶⁰ δεικνύετε, καὶ μὴ θέλοντες,⁶¹ τὸν Χριστὸν⁶² ἀληθεύοντα, τὸν εἰπόντα⁶³ ὅτι "ἔσεσθε μισούμενοι ὑπὸ πάντων διὰ τὸ ὄνομά μου."ᵈ οὐ μόνον 15 δὲ τοῦτο, ἀλλὰ καὶ ἃ εἶπεν ἡμῖν⁶⁴ ἅτινα θεωροῦμεν καθ' ἡμέραν⁶⁵ γινόμενα, καὶ ἐπιπλεῖον αὐτὸν ὡς θεὸν προσκυνοῦμεν.⁶⁶ εἶπεν ὅτι "κηρυχθήσεται τὸ εὐαγγέλιον ἐν ὅλῳ τῷ κόσμῳ."⁶⁷ᵉ εἶπεν ὅτι⁶⁸ "εἰ μὴ ἀφή-

⁴¹ τῆς πίστεως add. P, τῆς ἐκκλησίας add. An.
⁴² καὶ ἡ πίστις om. P.
⁴³ τὸν om. PAn.
⁴⁴ οὕτως add. PAn.
⁴⁵ εἰρηκότα P, ὁρίσαντα An.
⁴⁶ ὁ Διοκλιτιανός; P, ὁ Διοκλητιανός; An.
⁴⁷ ποῦ P.
⁴⁸ καὶ Μαξιμιανός om. et ποῦ ἐστὶν ὁ Νέρων; ποῦ ὁ Ὀυεσπασιανός; add. An.
⁴⁹ ἔστιν om. PAn.
⁵⁰ ποῦ ἔστιν Ὀυεσπασιανὸς om. PAn. ποῦ ὁ Μαξιμιανὸς add. An.
⁵¹ τοὺς τοῦ Χριστοῦ P, τοὺς Χριστοῦ An.   ⁵² κινήσαντες P.
⁵³ καὶ ἡ πίστις αὐτοῦ add. P.
⁵⁴ ἐπαύσατο P.
⁵⁵ καὶ πάλιν "ἐπὶ βασιλεῖς καὶ ἡγεμόνας ἀχθήσεσθε διὰ τὸ ὄνομά μου"ᶠ add. P, καὶ παλιν "ἐπὶ βασι-

λεῖς καὶ ἡγεμόνας ἀχθήσεσθε ἕνεκεν ἐμοῦ" add. An.
⁵⁶ ἢ μὴ μισεῖτε P, ἢ μισεῖτε An.
⁵⁷ μήτε om. P.
⁵⁸ μηδὲ P.
⁵⁹ μισεῖτε P.
⁶⁰ ἡμᾶς, μήτε ὑμεῖς κ.τ.λ. . . . . . . πάντως om. An.
⁶¹ βουλόμενοι P. καὶ μὴ θέλοντες om. An.
⁶² Χριστὸν θεὸν P.
⁶³ ἀληθεύοντα, τὸν εἰπόντα V, ἀληθεύοντα εἰπόντα ἡμῖν An., ἀληθινὸν προειπόντα ἡμῖν P.
⁶⁴ ἡμῖν om. PAn.
⁶⁵ καθ' ἡμέραν θεωροῦμεν PAn.
⁶⁶ προσκυνοῦμεν PAn., προσκυνούμενον V.
⁶⁷ εἶπεν ὅτι "οὐ μὴ μείνη λίθος ἐπὶ λίθον εἰς τὸν ναὸν ὑμῶν"ᵍ add. PAn.
⁶⁸ ὅτι om. PAn.

σεις⁶⁹ πατέρα καὶ μητέρα⁷⁰ καὶ ἀδελφοὺς⁷¹ οὐ δύνασαί⁷²
μοι ἀκολουθῆσαι."⁷³ʰ εἶπεν ἡμῖν μεταλαμβάνειν τοῦ
σώματος⁷⁴ καὶ αἵματος⁷⁵ αὐτοῦ.⁷⁶ⁱ εἶπεν ἡμῖν⁷⁷ περὶ
ἐλεημοσύνης κρυπτῶς αὐτὴν ποιεῖν.ᵏ εἶπεν ἡμῖν βαπτί-
5 ζεσθαι εἰς ὄνομα πατρὸς καὶ υἱοῦ καὶ ἁγίου πνεύματος.ˡ
εἶπεν ἡμῖν ὅτι " μεθ᾽ ὑμῶν εἰμὶ πάσας τὰς ἡμέρας ἕως
τῆς συντελείας τοῦ αἰῶνος."⁷⁸ᵐ τίς οὖν ἔστιν ὁ δυνά-
μενος ἐλέγξαι⁷⁹ ὅτι ταῦτα ἐψεύσατο⁸⁰ ἐν τούτοις ὁ Χριστὸς ἡμῶν; ⁸¹ οὐδείς. ἆρα οὐκ ἔπεσεν ὁ ναὸς⁸² καὶ ἐκαύ-
10 θη⁸³ ὑπὸ τῶν Ῥωμαίων;⁸⁴ ἆρα οὐκ ἐκηρύχθη τὸ εὐαγγέλιον αὐτοῦ⁸⁵ ἐν ὅλῳ τῷ κόσμῳ; ἆρα οὐ μισούμεθα οἱ
χριστιανοὶ⁸⁶ διὰ τὸ ὄνομα αὐτοῦ ὑπὸ πάντων;⁸⁷ ἆρα
οὐ θεωρεῖτε πολλοὺς καθ᾽ ἡμέραν βαπτιζομένους⁸⁸ εἰς
τὸ ὄνομα τοῦ πατρὸς καὶ τοῦ υἱοῦ καὶ τοῦ ἁγίου πνεύ-
15 ματος;⁸⁹ ἆρα οὐ βλέπομεν καὶ νοοῦμεν ὅτι μεθ᾽ ἡμῶν
ἐστιν ὁ Χριστὸς ἕως τῆς συντελείας τοῦ αἰῶνος, μὴ συγ-
χωρῶν καταργηθῆναι τὴν πίστιν ἡμῶν; ἆρα οὐ θεωροῦμεν μυρίους ἐξ ἡμῶν κρυπτῶς ποιοῦντας τὴν ἐλεημοσύνην
αὐτῶν κατὰ τὴν ἐντολὴν τοῦ Χριστοῦ;⁹⁰ τίς οὖν βλέπων
20 τὰ τοιαῦτα καὶ τοσαῦτα αὐτοῦ τοῦ Χριστοῦ ῥήματα καὶ

⁶⁹ ὁ μὴ ἀφίων PAn.
⁷⁰ καὶ μητέρα om. An.
⁷¹ καὶ ἀδελφᾶς add. An.
⁷² δύναται PAn.
⁷³ ἀκολουθῆσαί μοι PAn.
⁷⁴ τὸ σῶμα P.   ⁷⁵ τὸ αἷμα P.
⁷⁶ εἶπεν μεθ᾽ ἡμῶν εἶναι πᾶσας
τὰς ἡμέρας ἕως τῆς συντελείας τοῦ
αἰῶνος add. P.
⁷⁷ ἡμῖν om. P.
⁷⁸ εἶπεν ἡμῖν ὅτι κ.τ.λ. . . . . . αἰῶνος" om. P.
⁷⁹ αὐτὸν add. PAn.
⁸⁰ ταῦτα ἐψεύσατο V, ἐψεύσατο
ταῦτα An., ἐψεύσατο ἐν τούτοις P.   ⁸¹ ἡμῶν om. P.
⁸² ὑμῶν add. PAn.
⁸³ ἐκάη PAn.
⁸⁴ ὑπὸ τῶν Ῥωμαίων P, om. An.,
ὑπὸ τῶν Ἰουδαίων V.

⁸⁵ αὐτοῦ om. P.
⁸⁶ ὑπὸ πάντων add. PAn.
⁸⁷ ἆρα οὐ θεωροῦμεν καθ᾽ ἡμέραν
μυρίους ἀφέντας πατέρας καὶ μη-
τέρας, καὶ ἀποταββομένους τῷ
κόσμῳ καὶ ἀκολουθοῦντας τῷ
Χριστῷ; ἆρα οὐ θεωρεῖτε καθ᾽
ἡμέραν ποιοῦντας τοὺς χριστια-
νοὺς καθὼς προεῖπεν ἡμῖν ὁ Χριστὸς; add. P. ἆρα οὐ θεωροῦμεν
μυρίους ἀφιόντας πατέρας καὶ μη-
τέρας, καὶ ἀκολουθοῦντας τῷ
Χριστῷ; add. An.
⁸⁸ καθ᾽ ἡμέραν βαπτιζομένους
πολλοὺς P.
⁸⁹ ἆρα οὐ θεωρεῖτε πολλοὺς κ.τ.λ.
. . . . τοῦ ἁγίου πνεύματος; om.
An.
⁹⁰ ἆρα οὐ θεωροῦμεν μυρίους
κ.τ.λ. . . . . . . Χριστοῦ; om. An.

ʰ cf. Luke xiv. 26.   ˡ cf. Mark xiv. 22, etc.   ᵏ cf. Matt. vi. 1 ff.
ˡ cf. Matt. xxviii. 19.   ᵐ Ib. vers. 20.

πράγματα, ἅπερ πρὸ ἑξακοσίων ἐτῶν [91] προεῖπεν,[92] σήμερον[93] καὶ καθ' ἡμέραν[94] γινόμενα καὶ λάμποντα,[95] δύναται ἀπιστῆσαι ἢ σκανδαλισθῆναι[96] εἰς αὐτόν; μὴ γένοιτο. καὶ γὰρ ἅπαντα τὰ περὶ αὐτοῦ οἱ προφῆται ὑμῶν[97] προεκήρυξαν, ἀλλ' ὑμεῖς οὐκ ἐμβλέπετε.[98]

11. Ἐρώτησαν οἱ Ἰουδαῖοι·[1] εἰ οὖν ἄρα οἱ προφῆται ἡμῶν τὰ περὶ τοῦ Χριστοῦ σου προεῖπον,[2] διὰ τί οὐκ εἶπον προφανῶς ὅτι γινώσκετε[3] Ἰουδαῖοι ὅτι μέλλει ἐλθεῖν ὁ Χριστὸς καὶ παῦσαι τὸν νόμον καὶ τὰς θυσίας τοῦ νόμου;[4]

ὁ χριστιανὸς εἶπεν·[5] εἰ εἶπον οὕτως γυμνῶς τὸ πρᾶγμα, εὐθέως ἐλιθάζετε αὐτούς, λοιπὸν δὲ καὶ τὰς βίβλους αὐτῶν ὅλας ἐκαίετε, καὶ ἡμεῖς εἰς τοῦτο ἐβλαπτόμεθα· ἄρτι γὰρ ἀπὸ[6] τῶν προφητῶν ὑμῶν[7] καταισχύνομεν ὑμᾶς,[8] πάντα τὰ τοῦ Χριστοῦ ἐξ αὐτῶν παριστῶντες, καὶ ὑμᾶς ἐλέγχοντες.[9]

12. Ὁ γὰρ Δαβὶδ λέγει[1] " ἔκλινεν οὐρανοὺς καὶ κατέβη·"[a] ἰδοὺ ἡ κατάβασις.[2] Ἡσαΐας λέγει " ἰδοὺ ἡ παρθένος ἐν γαστρὶ ἕξει, καὶ τέξεται υἱόν, καὶ καλέσουσι τὸ ὄνομα αὐτοῦ Ἐμμανουήλ·"[b] ἰδοὺ ἡ γέννησις. " ὤρυξαν χεῖράς μου καὶ πόδας μου"[c] καὶ " ἔδωκαν εἰς τὸ βρῶμά μου χολήν, καὶ εἰς τὴν δίψαν μου ἐπότισάν με ὄξον,"[d] καὶ διεμερίσαντο τὰ ἱμάτιά μου ἑαυτοῖς, καὶ ἐπὶ τὸν ἱματισμόν μου ἔβαλον κλῆρον·"[e] ἰδοὺ[5] ἡ σταύρωσις.

[91] πρὸ πολλῶν ἐτῶν P, πρὸ χρόνων ὀκτακοσίων ἢ καὶ ἐπέκεινα An.
[92] προεῖπεν om. P.
[93] μέχρι τῆς σήμερον P.
[94] καὶ καθ' ἡμέραν om. P.
[95] ὑπὲρ ἥλιον add. P.
[96] ἀπιστῆσαι ἢ σκανδαλισθῆναι VAn., σκανδαλισθῆναι ἢ ἀπιστῆσαι P.
[97] ὑμῶν om. P.
[98] οὐ βλέπετε P. καὶ γὰρ ἅπαντα κ.τ.λ. .... οὐκ ἐμβλέπετε om. An.
[1] Ἐρώτημα Ἰουδαίου P, ΤΟΥ ΑΥΤΟΥ ΔΕΥΤΕΡΑ ΕΡΩΤΗΣΙΣ An.
[2] εἶπον P.
[3] ἴδετε P, ἵνα εἰδῆτε An.
[4] τοῦ νόμου om. P.

[5] εἶπεν om. P.
[6] ἐκ PAn.
[7] ὑμῶν om. P.
[8] ὑμᾶς καταισχύνομεν PAn.
[9] πάντα τὰ τοῦ Χριστοῦ κ.τ.λ. .... ἐλέγχοντες V, ὅλα τὰ τοῦ Χριστοῦ ἐξ αὐτῶν ὑμᾶς ἐλέγχοντες καὶ παριστῶντες An., ἐλέγχοντες ὑμᾶς ἐξ αὐτῶν καὶ παριστῶντες τὴν ἀλήθειαν P.

[1] ὁ Δαβὶδ μὲν γὰρ λέγει An.
[2] ἰδοὺ ἡ κατάβασις om. An.
[3] καὶ " ἔδωκαν εἰς τὸ βρῶμά μου κ.τ.λ. ..... ὄξον " om. An.
[4] ἐξηρίθμησαν πάντα τὰ ὀστᾶ μου add. An.
[5] ἰδοὺ καὶ An.

[a] Psa. xvii. 10.   [b] Isa. vii. 14.   [c] Psa. xxi. 17.
[d] Psa. lxviii. 22.   [e] Psa. xxi. 19.

ἆρα ἐψεύσαντο οἱ εὐαγγελισταὶ ἡμῶν εἰπόντες ὅτι ἔπαθε ταῦτα ὁ Χριστός; ἐὰν ἐψεύσαντο καὶ Δαβὶδ ἐψεύσατο ὁ ταῦτα εἰπών· ἀλλὰ μὴ γένοιτο. θέλεις ἀκοῦσαι καὶ τὴν ἀνάστασιν αὐτοῦ; Ὡσηὲ ὁ προφήτης
5 λέγει " ζητήσωμεν τὸν κύριον, καὶ ὑγιάσει ἡμᾶς μετὰ δύο ἡμέρας· καὶ ἐν τῇ τρίτῃ ἡμέρᾳ ἀναστησόμεθα."[f]

[12.[1] Λέγει γὰρ ὁ Δαβὶδ "ἔκλινεν οὐρανοὺς καὶ κατέβη·"[a] καὶ πάλιν "καταβήσεται ὡς ὑετὸς ἐπὶ πόκον·"[b] ἰδοὺ ἡ κατάβασις. ὁμοίως καὶ Ἡσαΐας λέγει "ἰδοὺ ἡ
10 παρθένος ἐν γαστρὶ ἕξει, καὶ τέξει υἱόν, καὶ καλέσουσι τὸ ὄνομα αὐτοῦ Ἐμμανουήλ·"[c] ἰδοὺ ἡ γέννησις. καὶ πάλιν ἀλλαχοῦ ὁ αὐτὸς προφήτης λέγει "οὐκ ἄγγελος, οὐ πρέσβυς, ἀλλ' αὐτὸς ὁ κύριος ἥξει καὶ σώσει ἡμᾶς·"[d] ὅτι δὲ θεός ἐστι, λέγει "καὶ καλεῖται τὸ ὄνομα αὐτοῦ
15 μεγάλης βουλῆς ἄγγελος, θεὸς ἰσχυρός, ἐξουσιαστής, ἄρχων εἰρήνης, πατὴρ τοῦ μέλλοντος αἰῶνος."[e] εἶτα καὶ τὸν τόπον τῆς γεννήσεως δηλῶν λέγει "γῆ Ζαβουλὼν καὶ γῆ Νεφθαλήμ, ὁδὸν θαλάσσης πέραν τοῦ Ἰορδάνου, Γαλιλαία τῶν ἐθνῶν. ὁ λαὸς ὁ καθήμενος
20 ἐν σκότει εἶδεν φῶς μέγα,"[f] τουτέστιν ὁ λαὸς τῶν ἐθνῶν τὸν Χριστὸν ἐκεῖ γεννηθέντα ἐδόξασαν καὶ προσεκύνησαν. καὶ Μιχαίας δὲ ὁ προφήτης οὕτως λέγει "καὶ σὺ Βηθλεέμ, γῆ Ἰούδα, οὐδαμῶς ἐλαχίστη εἶ ἐν τοῖς ἡγεμόσιν Ἰούδα· ἐκ σοῦ γὰρ ἐξελεύσεται ἡγού-
25 μενος."[g] καὶ Δαβὶδ δὲ δεικνὺς ὅτι διὰ τὰ ἔθνη ὁ θεὸς σαρκοῦσθαι ἔμελλεν, τρανῶς καὶ ἀνυποστόλως εἶπεν "ἐβασίλευσεν ὁ θεὸς ἐπὶ τὰ ἔθνη·"[h] καὶ πάλιν ὡς ἐκ προσώπου τοῦ πατρὸς πρὸς τὸν υἱὸν φησὶν "αἴτησαι παρ' ἐμοῦ, καὶ δώσω σοι ἔθνη τὴν κληρονομίαν σου·"[i]
30 καὶ πάλιν "πάντα τὰ ἔθνη κροτήσατε χεῖρας,"[k] "ὅτι παιδίον ἐγεννήθη ἡμῖν, υἱὸς καὶ ἐδόθη ἡμῖν·"[l] καὶ "πάντα τὰ ἔθνη ὅσα ἐποίησας ἥξουσιν καὶ προσκυνήσουσιν ἐνώπιόν σου κύριε."[m] ὅτι δὲ ἐν Σιὼν ἔμελλεν φανεροῦσθαι ὁ Χριστός, καὶ ὅτι ὕψιστός ἐστιν, ἐν τῷ
35 πς' ψαλμῷ οὕτως Δαβὶδ προεφήτευσεν, "μήτηρ Σιὼν

[1] Usque ad caput 13, pag. 73 P; totum om. V.

[f] Hos. vi. 1-2.   [a] Psa. xvii. 10.   [b] Psa. lxxi. 6.   [c] Isa. vii. 14.
[d] Isa. lxiii. 9.   [e] Isa. ix. 6.   [f] Isa. ix. 1-2.   [g] Mic. v. 2.
[h] Psa. xlvi. 9.   [i] ii. 8.   [k] xlvi. 1.   [l] Isa. ix. 6.
[m] Psa. lxxxv. 9.

ἐρεῖ ἄνθρωπος, καὶ ἄνθρωπος ἐγεννήθη ἐν αὐτῇ, καὶ
αὐτὸς ἐθεμελίωσεν αὐτὴν ὁ ὕψιστος·"ⁿ ὥστε οὖν
ὕψιστός ἐστιν ὁ Χριστὸς καὶ υἱὸς τοῦ θεοῦ. ὅτι δὲ
τεχθεὶς ὁ Χριστὸς ἔμελλεν μετὰ τῆς ἰδίας μητρὸς τῆς
πνευματικῆς νεφέλης ἔρχεσθαι εἰς Ἄιγυπτον, Ἡσαΐου 5
τοῦ προφήτου ἀκούσωμεν λέγοντος, " ἰδοὺ κύριος κάθη-
ται ἐπὶ νεφέλης κούφης, καὶ ἥξει εἰς Ἄιγυπτον καὶ σεισ-
θήσονται τὰ χειροποίητα Ἀιγύπτου."ᵒ ὅτι δὲ βαπτιζο-
μένου τοῦ Χριστοῦ ἔμελλεν ὁ πατὴρ ἄνωθεν αὐτῷ
μαρτυρεῖν, ἐν τῷ κη΄ ψαλμῷ οὕτως γέγραπται, " φωνὴ 10
κυρίου ἐπὶ τῶν ὑδάτων, ὁ θεὸς τῆς δόξης ἐβρόντησε,
κύριος ἐπὶ ὑδάτων πολλῶν."ᴾ εἶτα καὶ περὶ τῶν θαυ-
μάτων αὐτοῦ καὶ ἰάσεων ὧν ἐποίησεν Ἡσαΐας ὁ προφήτης λέγει " αὐτὸς τὰς ἀσθενίας ἡμῶν ἀνέλαβεν καὶ
τὰς νόσους ἐβάστασεν."ᑫ ὅτι δὲ εἰρηνεῦσαι τὸν κόσ- 15
μον ἦλθεν, ἀκούσωμεν τοῦ Δαβὶδ λέγοντος, " ἀνατελεῖ
ἐν ταῖς ἡμέραις αὐτοῦ δικαιοσύνη, καὶ πλῆθος εἰρήνης
ἕως οὗ ἀνταναιρεθῇ ἡ σελήνη. καὶ κατακυριεύσει ἀπὸ
θαλάσσης ἕως θαλάσσης, καὶ ἀπὸ ποταμῶν ἕως περά-
των τῆς οἰκουμένης."ʳ κἂν εἴπῃς, ὦ Ἰουδαῖε, ὅτι περὶ 20
Σολομῶντος λέγει ψεύδῃ σε, προϊὼν γὰρ λέγει " πρὸ
τοῦ ἡλίου διαμενεῖ τὸ ὄνομα αὐτοῦ, καὶ πάντα τὰ
ἔθνη μακαριοῦσιν αὐτόν,"ˢ καὶ " προσκυνήσουσιν αὐτὸν πάντες οἱ βασιλεῖς τῆς γῆς."ᵗ ταῦτα δὲ οὐ δυνα-
τὸν εἰς Σολομῶντα λέγεσθαι, οὐδὲ γὰρ ἦν πρὸ τοῦ 25
ἡλίου, ἀλλ' οὔτε διήρκεσεν ἕως οὗ ἀνταναιρεθῇ ἡ σελήνη. ὅτι δὲ καὶ διὰ βαπτίσματος ἔμελλεν Χριστὸς ὁ
θεὸς ἡμῶν καταργεῖν τὸν διάβολον καὶ τοὺς σὺν αὐτῷ
δαίμονας, ὁ Δαβὶδ λέγει μαρτυρῶν πρὸς αὐτὸν οὕτως,
" σὺ συνέτριψας τὰς κεφαλὰς τῶν δρακόντων ἐπὶ τοῦ 30
ὕδατος· σὺ συνέθλασας τὴν κεφαλὴν τοῦ δράκοντος."ᵘ
ὅτι δὲ ποιητής ἐστιν οὐρανοῦ καὶ γῆς ὁ ἐν θαλάσσῃ
περιπατήσας, τοῦ Ἰὼβ ἀκούσωμεν λέγοντος " ὁ τανύσας
τὸν οὐρανὸν μόνος, καὶ περιπατῶν ἐπὶ θαλάσσης ὡς
ἐπὶ ἐδάφους."ᵛ περὶ δὲ τοῦ πώλου καὶ τῆς ὄνου ἐφ' ὧν ὁ 35
Χριστὸς ἐκάθισεν, ἀκούσωμεν Ζαχαρίου τοῦ προφήτου
λέγοντος " χαῖρε σφόδρα, θύγατερ Σιὼν, κήρυσσε,

ⁿ Psa. lxxxvi. 5.   ᵒ Isa. xix. 1.   ᴾ Psa. xxviii. 3.
ᑫ Isa. liii. 4.   ʳ Psa. lxxi. 7-8.   ˢ Ib. vers. 17.
ᵗ Ib. vers. 11.   ᵘ Psa. lxxiii. 13-14.   ᵛ Job ix. 8.

Θύγατερ Ἱερουσαλήμ· ἰδοὺ ὁ βασιλεύς σου ἔρχεταί σοι πραΰς καὶ σώζων, ἐπιβεβηκὼς ἐπὶ πῶλον ὄνου υἱὸν ὑποζυγίου."ʷ τί τοίνυν τῶν προφητικῶν τούτων φωνῶν τηλαυγέσ-
5 τερον; ἀλλ' ὅμως καίπερ οὕτως τρανῶς περὶ τοῦ Χριστοῦ τῶν προφητῶν προφητευσάντων, ἀπετύφλωσεν ὁ σατανᾶς τὰ τῶν Ἰουδαίων ὄμματα, καὶ ἐπώρωσεν τὰς τῆς ψυχῆς αὐτῶν ἀκοὰς, ἵνα τὰς τοιαύτας ἀληθεῖς μαρτυρίας παραγράψονται. καὶ τοῦτο δῆλον καὶ ἀναμφί-
10 βολον ἐκ τῶν τοῦ Ἡσαΐου ῥημάτων λέγοντος "κύριε, τίς ἐπίστευσε τῇ ἀκοῇ ἡμῶν; καὶ ὁ βραχίων κυρίου τίνι ἀπεκαλύφθη;"ˣ διὰ τοῦτο οὐκ ἠδύναντο πιστεύειν ὅτι πάλιν εἶπεν Ἡσαΐας "τετύφλωκεν αὐτῶν τοὺς ὀφθαλμοὺς καὶ πεπώρωκεν αὐτῶν τὴν καρδίαν, ἵνα μὴ ἴδωσι
15 τοῖς ὀφθαλμοῖς καὶ νοήσωσιν τῇ καρδίᾳ καὶ ἐπιστραφῶσιν καὶ ἰάσομαι αὐτούς."ʸ βλέπεις πῶς πανταχοῦ αὐτοὶ αἴτιοι τῆς ἀπιστίας καὶ ἀπωλείας αὐτῶν καθεστήκασιν. τοῦτο γὰρ ἠνήξατο εἰπὼν "κύριε, τίς ἐπίστευσε τῇ ἀκοῇ ἡμῶν;"ᶻ περὶ Ἰουδαίων τοῦτο εἴρηκε,
20 οὐ περὶ τῶν ἐξ ἐθνῶν. ὅτι δὲ ἀληθές ἐστι τὸ εἰρημένον μαρτυρεῖ Δαβὶδ λέγων "πάντα τὰ ἔθνη ὅσα ἐποίησας ἥξουσι καὶ προσκυνήσουσιν ἐνώπιόν σου, κύριε,"ᵃᵃ καὶ τὰ ἑξῆς. ἀκούσωμεν δὲ καὶ περὶ τῶν παίδων τῶν ἀπαντησάντων τῷ κυρίῳ καὶ βοησάντων τὸ ὡσαννὰ καὶ
25 κύριον αὐτὸν ἀποκαλεσάντων, πῶς καὶ τοῦτο Δαβὶδ προεφήτευσε, λέγων ἐν τῷ ψαλμῷ, "κύριε, ὁ κύριος ἡμῶν, ὡς θαυμαστὸν τὸ ὄνομά σου ἐν πάσῃ τῇ γῇ· ὅτι ἐπήρθη ἡ μεγαλοπρέπειά σου ὑπεράνω τῶν οὐρανῶν. ἐκ στόματος νηπίων καὶ θηλαζόντων κατηρτίσω αἶ-
30 νον."ᵇᵇ τί πρὸς τοῦτο ἔχεις ἀντειπεῖν, ὦ Ἰουδαῖε;
περὶ δὲ τῆς τοῦ Ἰούδα προδοσίας ἐν τῷ μ' ψαλμῷ λέγει "ὁ ἐσθίων ἄρτους μου ἐμεγάλυνεν ἐπ' ἐμὲ πτερνισμόν."ᶜᶜ τὴν δὲ τῶν Ἰουδαίων καὶ Ἡρώδου καὶ Πιλάτου ἐπιβουλὴν κατὰ Χριστοῦ ὁ β' ψαλμὸς λέγει "ἵνα τί
35 ἐφρύαξαν ἔθνη, καὶ λαοὶ ἐμελέτησαν κενά; παρέστησαν οἱ βασιλεῖς τῆς γῆς," τουτέστιν Πιλᾶτος καὶ Ἡρώδης, "καὶ οἱ ἄρχοντες συνήχθησαν ἐπὶ τὸ αὐτό,""Ἄννας καὶ Καϊάφας καὶ οἱ λοιποὶ ἀρχιερεῖς καὶ γραμματεῖς, "κατὰ τοῦ κυρίου καὶ κατὰ τοῦ χριστοῦ αὐτοῦ."ᵈᵈ πάντως

ʷ Zech. ix. 9.   ˣ Isa. liii. 1.   ʸ Isa. vi. 10.   ᶻ Isa. liii. 1.
ᵃᵃ Psa. lxxxv. 9.   ᵇᵇ viii. 2–3.   ᶜᶜ xl. 10.   ᵈᵈ Psa. ii. 1–2.

ἤκουσες ὅτι "κατὰ τοῦ κυρίου καὶ κατὰ τοῦ χριστοῦ αὐτοῦ," ὁ γὰρ πολεμῶν τὸν υἱὸν ὑβρίζει τὸν πατέρα. ἔχεις ἀναισχυντεῖν κἂν ἐπὶ τοῦτο, ὦ Ἰουδαῖε; περὶ δὲ τῶν δεσμῶν ὧν ἔδωσαν τὸν Χριστὸν, ταλανίζων τοὺς Ἰουδαίους, Ἡσαΐας ὁ προφήτης λέγει " οὐαὶ τῇ ψυχῇ αὐτῶν διότι βεβουλεύονται βουλὴν πονηρὰν καθ᾿ ἑαυτῶν, λέγοντες, δήσωμεν τὸν δίκαιον ὅτι δύσχριστος ἡμῖν ἐστιν."ee ἐρώτησον λοιπὸν τὸν Ἰουδαῖον καὶ εἰπὲ αὐτῷ, τίς ἀνθρώπων ἐπὶ τῆς γῆς ἀναμάρτητος; εὔδηλον ὅτι οὐδείς· λέγει γὰρ προφανῶς ἡ γραφὴ ὅτι " οὐδεὶς καθαρὸς ἀπὸ ῥύπου, οὐδ᾿ ἂν μία ἡμέρα ἡ ζωὴ αὐτοῦ ἐπὶ τῆς γῆς."ff καὶ πάλιν φησὶν ὁ προφήτης πρὸς τὸν θεὸν " μὴ εἰσέλθῃς εἰς κρίσιν μετὰ τοῦ δούλου σου, ὅτι οὐ δικαιωθήσεται ἐνώπιόν σου πᾶς ζῶν·"gg ὥστε φανερῶς διδασκόμεθα ὅτι οὐδεὶς ἀναμάρτητος εἰ μὴ εἷς ὁ θεός. ἀκούσωμεν οὖν τί λοιπὸν ὁ προφήτης Ἡσαΐας διαλέγεται ἡμῖν περὶ τοῦ πάθους τοῦ ἀναμαρτήτου χριστοῦ τοῦ θεοῦ, " ὡς πρόβατον ἐπὶ σφαγὴν ἤχθη, καὶ ὡς ἀμνὸς ἐναντίον τοῦ κείραντος αὐτὸν ἄφωνος, οὗτος οὐκ ἀνοίγει τὸ στόμα αὐτοῦ·"hh δῆλον δὲ ὅτι ἐσιώπα ὁ Χριστὸς Πιλάτῳ παριστάμενος ἐπὶ τὸ πάθος αὐτοῦ· " ἐν τῇ ταπεινώσει αὐτοῦ ἡ κρίσις αὐτοῦ ἤρθη· τὴν δὲ γενεὰν αὐτοῦ τίς διηγήσεται,"ii τουτέστιν τὴν προαιώνιον γέννησιν· κατὰ σάρκα γὰρ γενεαλογεῖται Χριστὸς ὁ θεός. εἶτα πάλιν " ἀπὸ τῶν ἀνομιῶν τοῦ λαοῦ μου ἥκει εἰς θάνατον·"kk δῆλον δὲ ὅτι ὑπὲρ τῶν ἁμαρτιῶν τοῦ κόσμου Χριστὸς ἀπέθανεν· " καὶ δώσω τοὺς πονηροὺς ἀντὶ τῆς ταφῆς αὐτοῦ," δῆλον ὅτι τοὺς Ἰουδαίους παραδοὺς τοῖς Ῥωμαίοις, " καὶ τοὺς πλουσίους ἀντὶ τοῦ θανάτου αὐτοῦ·"ll διὰ τί; ὦ προφῆτα, εἰπὲ ἡμῖν· " ὅτι ἁμαρτίαν" φησὶν " οὐκ ἐποίησεν, οὐδὲ δόλος εὑρέθη ἐν τῷ στόματι αὐτοῦ."ll τίς ἄνθρωπος ὡς πρόβατον ἐπὶ σφαγὴν ἤχθη, ἁμαρτίαν μὴ ποιήσας; ἀλλ᾿ οὐκ ἔχουσι δεῖξαι ἄνθρωπον ἀναμάρτητον, εἰ μὴ μόνον τὸν θεὸν τὸν γενόμενον ἄνθρωπον. ἀκούσωμεν δὲ καὶ περὶ τῶν ψευδομαρτύρων τῶν κατὰ τοῦ Χριστοῦ ψευδομαρτυρισάντων ἐν ψαλμῷ λδ´ " ἀναστάντες μοι μάρτυρες ἄδικοι ἃ οὐκ ἐγίνωσκον ἠρώτων με· ἀνταπεδίδοσάν μοι πονηρὰ ἀντὶ ἀγαθῶν."mm δῆλον

ee Isa. iii. 9-10.　ff Job xiv. 4-5.　gg Psa. cxlii. 2.　hh Isa. liii. 7.
ii vers. 8.　kk Ibid.　ll vers. 9.　mm Psa. xxxiv. 11-12.

ὅτι ὧν ὁ Χριστὸς ἐν τῷ λαῷ παντὶ πεποίηκεν πρῶτον
μὲν τὴν ἔξοδον αὐτῶν τὴν ἐξ Αἰγύπτου καὶ τὰ λοιπὰ
μυρία ἀγαθὰ ἃ εἰς αὐτοὺς εἰργάσατο, ἔπειτα δὲ καὶ
τοὺς νοσοῦντας αὐτῶν ἰασάμενος. περὶ δὲ τῶν μαστι-
5 γωσάντων καὶ ῥαπισάντων τὸν Χριστὸν Ἡσαΐας ὁ προφήτης ὡς ἐκ προσώπου τοῦ χριστοῦ οὕτως ἔφη, "τὸν
νῶτόν μου δέδωκα εἰς μάστιγας, τὰς δὲ σιαγόνας μου εἰς
ῥαπίσματα, τὸ δὲ πρόσωπόν μου οὐκ ἀπέστρεψα ἀπὸ
αἰσχύνης ἐμπτυσμάτων."[nn] ὁμοίως δὲ καὶ ὁ προφήτης
10 Δαβὶδ ἐκ προσώπου τοῦ χριστοῦ ἐν λζ´ ψαλμῷ λέγει ὅτι
"ἐγὼ εἰς μάστιγας ἕτοιμος, καὶ ἡ ἀλγηδών μου ἐνώπιόν
μου ἔστιν διὰ παντός."[oo] περὶ δὲ τῆς πράσεως τοῦ Χριστοῦ λέγει Ἰερεμίας ὁ προφήτης "καὶ ἔλαβον τὰ τριάκοντα
ἀργύρια τὴν τιμὴν τοῦ τετιμημένου ὃν ἐτιμήσαντο ἀπὸ
15 υἱῶν Ἰσραὴλ, καὶ ἔδωκα αὐτὰ εἰς τὸν ἀγρὸν τοῦ κεραμέως, καθὰ συνέταξέν μοι κύριος."[pp] ἆρα τοῦτο παρα-
γράψασθαι δύνασθε, ὦ Ἰουδαῖοι, ὅπερ πρὸ ὀφθαλμῶν
παντὸς τοῦ κόσμου πρόκειται ἐκ τότε καὶ μέχρι τοῦ νῦν;
λέγω δὴ ὁ ἀγρὸς τοῦ κεραμέως εἰς ταφὴν τοῖς ξένοις.
20 ὡσαύτως δὲ καὶ Ζαχαρίας ὁ προφήτης περὶ τῶν λ´ ἀρ-
γυρίων ὡς ἐκ προσώπου τοῦ χριστοῦ "καὶ ἔτησαν
τὸν μισθόν μου τριάκοντα ἀργυρίους."[qq] ὅτι δὲ τὴν
ἀρχὴν τῆς σωτηρίας ἡμῶν ἢ γοῦν τὸν τίμιον σταυρὸν
ἐν τοῖς ἰδίοις αὐτοῦ ὤμοις ἐβάστασεν ὁ Χριστὸς ὑψω-
25 θεὶς ἐν αὐτῷ, Ἡσαΐας προεφήτευσε, λέγων "οὗ ἡ ἀρχὴ
ἐπὶ τοῦ ὤμου αὐτοῦ,"[rr] τουτέστιν ὁ ζωοποιὸς σταυρός.
περὶ δὲ τοῦ ἐξ ἀκανθῶν στεφάνου γέγραπται ἐν
τοῖς ᾄσμασι τῶν ᾀσμάτων οὕτως, "θυγατέρες Ἱερουσαλὴμ, ἐξέλθατε καὶ ἴδετε τὸν στέφανον ὃν ἐστεφά-
30 νωσεν αὐτὸν ἡ μήτηρ αὐτοῦ,"[ss] τουτέστιν ἡ συναγωγὴ
τῶν Ἰουδαίων, μήτηρ γὰρ Χριστοῦ αὕτη κατὰ σάρκα
νοεῖται, "ἐν ἡμέρᾳ νυμφεύσεως αὐτοῦ καὶ ἐν ἡμέρᾳ
εὐφροσύνης καρδίας αὐτοῦ·"[ss] πρόδηλον δὲ ὅτι ἡ ἡμέρα
τοῦ πάθους τοῦ χριστοῦ ἡμέρα ἦν εὐφροσύνης αὐτοῦ
35 διὰ τὴν σωτηρίαν ἡμῶν· ὥσπερ γὰρ ἄκανθαί τινες
οὕτως ὑπῆρχον αἱ ἁμαρτίαι τοῦ κόσμου ἅστινας ἐλθὼν
ὁ χριστὸς "ὁ ἀμνὸς τοῦ θεοῦ ὁ αἴρων τὴν ἁμαρτίαν
τοῦ κόσμου"[tt] ἐξήλειψεν. καὶ καθάπερ διὰ τοῦ καρ-
ποῦ τοῦ ξύλου ἡ ἁμαρτία τὴν εἴσοδον ἔσχεν, οὕτως

[nn] Isa. l. 6.   [oo] Psa. xxxvii. 18.   [pp] Zech. xi. 12-13.   [qq] Ib. vers. 12.
[rr] Isa. ix. 6.   [ss] Cant. iii. 11.   [tt] John i. 29.

διὰ τοῦ σταυροῦ τοῦ κόσμου ἡ σωτηρία καὶ διὰ τοῦτο
ἐν κήπῳ τὸ πάθος τοῦ Χριστοῦ ἐγένετο. ἐπειδὴ ἐν παρα-
δείσῳ παρέβη ὁ Ἀδὰμ διὸ καὶ τῷ λῃστῇ παράδεισος
ἀπὸ τοῦ σταυροῦ ἀνοίγεται. διὰ τοῦτο δὲ καὶ ὥρᾳ
ἕκτῃ ὁ Χριστὸς σταυροῦται ἐπειδὴ τὸ δειλινὸν ὁ Ἀδὰμ 5
ἐξορίσθη. χολῆς δὲ γεύεται ἵνα τὴν γλυκύτητα τῆς
πικρᾶς ἡδονῆς τοῦ Ἀδὰμ ἰάσηται. ῥαπίζεται ἵνα ἐμοὶ
τὴν ἐλευθερίαν χαρίσηται. ἐμπτύεται ἵνα τὸ ἐμφύ-
σημα τοῦ ἁγίου πνεύματος ἡμῖν δωρήσηται. φραγελ-
λοῦται ἵνα τὸ ἐπὶ τοῦ νώτου ἡμῶν φορτίον τῶν ἁμαρ- 10
τιῶν σκορπίσῃ.¹ γυμνοῦται ἐν ξύλῳ ἵνα τὴν ἐμὴν
αἰσχύνην σκεπάσῃ.² θανατοῦται ἵνα ἐμὲ ζωοποιήσῃ.³
κατακρίνεται ἵνα ἐμὲ τῆς κατάρας ἀπολύσῃ. καλάμῃ
τὴν κεφαλὴν τύπτεται ἵνα τὴν τοῦ ὄφεως κεφαλὴν
συντρίψῃ.⁴ λόγχῃ τὴν πλευρὰν νύττεται ἵνα τὴν ἐκ 15
πλευρᾶς τοῦ Ἀδὰμ κτησθεῖσαν γυναῖκα θεραπεύσῃ,⁵
καὶ τὴν φλογίνην ῥομφαίαν τὴν καθ᾿ ἡμῶν στρεφο-
μένην παύσῃ,⁶ καὶ τὴν ὁδὸν ἡμῖν τοῦ παραδείσου ἀν-
οίξῃ.⁷ ὅτι δὲ ἐν μέσῳ τῆς γῆς ἔμελλεν ὁ χριστὸς σταυροῦσθαι ἐν τῷ ογʹ ψαλμῷ λέγει οὕτως ὁ Δαβίδ, "ὁ δὲ 20
θεὸς βασιλεὺς ἡμῶν πρὸ αἰῶνος εἰργάσατο σωτηρίαν
ἐν μέσῳ τῆς γῆς." ᵘᵘ ὅτι δὲ μετὰ λῃστῶν ἔμελλεν ὁ χριστὸς σταυροῦσθαι Ἡσαΐας ὁ προφήτης φησὶ "καὶ μετὰ
ἀνόμων ἐλογίσθη." ᵛᵛ περὶ δὲ τῶν ἥλων καὶ τοῦ διαμε-
ρισμοῦ τῶν ἱματίων ἐν ψαλμῷ καʹ οὕτως γέγραπται, 25
"ὤρυξαν χεῖράς μου καὶ πόδας μου, ἐξηρίθμησαν
πάντα τὰ ὀστᾶ μου·" ʷʷ καὶ "διεμερίσαντο τὰ ἱμάτιά μου ἑαυτοῖς, καὶ ἐπὶ τὸν ἱματισμόν μου ἔβαλον
κλῆρον." ˣˣ ὁμοίως δὲ καὶ Ζαχαρίας ὁ προφήτης περὶ
τῶν ἥλων οὕτως ἔφη, "καὶ ἐροῦσιν πρὸς αὐτόν, τί 30
αἱ πληγαὶ αὗται αἱ ἀνὰ μέσον τῶν χειρῶν σου; καὶ
ἐρεῖ, ἃς ἐπλήγην ἐν τῷ οἴκῳ τῷ ἀγαπητῷ μου." ʸʸ
περὶ δὲ τοῦ σκοτασμοῦ ὁ αὐτὸς προφήτης Ζαχαρίας
λέγει "καὶ ἔσται ἐν ἐκείνῃ τῇ ἡμέρᾳ οὐκ ἔσται φῶς,
καὶ ψῦχος καὶ πάγος ἔσται μία ἡμέρα, καὶ ἡμέρα ἐκείνη 35

---

¹ σκορπίσει cod. ⁴ συντρίψει cod.
² σκεπάσει cod. ⁵ θεραπεύσει cod.
³ ζωοποιήσει cod. ⁶ παύσει cod. ⁷ ἀνοίξει cod.

ᵘᵘ Psa. lxxiii. 12. ᵛᵛ Isa. liii. 12. ʷʷ Psa. xxi. 17-18.
ˣˣ vers. 19. ʸʸ Zech. xiii. 6.

γνωστὴ τῷ κυρίῳ, καὶ οὐχ ἡμέρα καὶ νὺξ, καὶ πρὸς ἑσπέραν ἔσται φῶς·"ᵃᵃ ὁμοίως δὲ καὶ Ἀμῶς ὁ προφήτης λέγει "καὶ ἔσται ἐν ἐκείνῃ τῇ ἡμέρᾳ, λέγει κύριος κύριος, καὶ δύσεται ὁ ἥλιος μεσημβρίας, καὶ συσκοτάσει ἐπὶ γῆς ἐν ἡμέρᾳ τὸ φῶς."ᵃᵃᵃ καὶ Ἰωὴλ ὁ προφήτης λέγει" ὁ ἥλιος καὶ ἡ σελήνη συσκοτάσουσιν, καὶ οἱ ἀστέρες δύσουσι. τὸ φέγγος αὐτῶν, καὶ κύριος δώσει φωνὴν αὐτοῦ."ᵇᵇᵇ ὅτι δὲ ἔμελλον ὄξος καὶ χολὴν ποτίζειν τὸν χριστὸν, ψαλμοῦ ξη' ἀκούσωμεν λέγοντος "ἔδωκαν εἰς τὸ βρῶμά μου χολὴν, καὶ εἰς τὴν δίψαν μου ἐπότισάν με ὄξος·"ᶜᶜᶜ ἰδοὺ καὶ ἡ σταύρωσις καὶ τὰ ἐν αὐτῇ παρακολουθήσαντα. διὸ ὁ αὐτὸς προφήτης τούτοις τὰ μέλλοντα προλέγει, "γενηθήτω ἡ τράπεζα αὐτῶν ἐνώπιον αὐτῶν εἰς παγίδα, καὶ εἰς ἀνταπόδοσιν, καὶ εἰς σκάνδαλον· σκοτισθήτωσαν οἱ ὀφθαλμοὶ αὐτῶν τοῦ μὴ βλέπειν, καὶ τὸν νῶτον αὐτῶν διὰ παντὸς σύνκαμψον."ᵈᵈᵈ καὶ διὰ τοῦ προφήτου Ἀββακοὺμᵃ ἀπειλεῖ ὁ θεὸς τοῖς οὕτω διακειμένουσιν, καὶ μὴ πιστεύουσιν, λέγων οὕτως, "ἴδετε οἱ καταφρονηταὶ καὶ ἐπιβλέψατε, καὶ θαυμάσατε, ὅτι ἔργον ἐργάζομαι ἐγὼ ἐν ταῖς ἡμέραις ὑμῶν, ὃ οὐ μὴ πιστεύσητε ἐάν τις ὑμῖν ἐκδιηγεῖται."ᵉᵉᵉ πάντα τοίνυν τοῖς Ἰουδαίοις ἁρμόζει, ὡς καὶ Μωϋσῆς τούτοις ἐπεμβαίνει, λέγων "καὶ ἔσται ἡ ζωή σου κρεμαμένη ἀπέναντι τῶν ὀφθαλμῶν σου, καὶ φοβηθήσῃ ἡμέρας καὶ νυκτὸς, καὶ οὐ πιστεύσεις τῇ ζωῇ σου."ᶠᶠᶠ περὶ δὲ τῆς ἐκκεντήσεως τῆς λόγχης λέγει Ζαχαρίας ὁ προφήτης "καὶ ἐπιβλέψονται πρός με εἰς ὃν ἐξεκέντησαν."ᵍᵍᵍ περὶ δὲ τῆς ἁγίας αὐτοῦ πλευρᾶς τῆς ἐκβλυσάσης τὸ αἷμα καὶ τὸ ὕδωρ ὁ αὐτὸς προφήτης λέγει "ἐν τῇ ἡμέρᾳ ἐκείνῃ ἐξελεύσεται ὕδωρ ζῶν ἐξ Ἱερουσαλήμ."ʰʰʰ ἀκούσομεν δὲ καὶ τοῦ προφήτου Ἡσαΐου περὶ τῆς ταφῆς τοῦ κυρίου λέγοντος, καὶ ὅπως διαγελᾷ τοὺς Ἰουδαίους, "ἴδετε ὡς ὁ δίκαιος ἀπώλετο, καὶ οὐδεὶς ἐκδέχεται τῇ καρδίᾳ,"ⁱⁱⁱ ἢ γοῦν τὴν αὐτοῦ ἀνάστασιν· καὶ πάλιν "ἀπὸ προσώπου ἀδικίας ἦρται ὁ δίκαιος καὶ ἔσται ἐν εἰρήνῃ ἡ ταφὴ αὐτοῦ·"ᵏᵏᵏ εἰρήνην

ᵃ Ἀμβακούμ cod.

ᶻᶻ Zech. xlv. 6-7.　ᵃᵃᵃ Amos viii. 9.　ᵇᵇᵇ Joel iii. 15.　ᶜᶜᶜ Psa. lxviii. 22.
ᵈᵈᵈ vers. 23-24.　ᵉᵉᵉ Hab. i. 5.　ᶠᶠᶠ Deut. xxviii. 66.　ᵍᵍᵍ Zech. xii. 10.
ʰʰʰ xiv. 8.　ⁱⁱⁱ Isa. lvii. 1.　ᵏᵏᵏ vers. 1-2.

δὲ λέγει ὅτε Πιλᾶτος μετ' εἰρήνης παρέδωκεν τὸ σῶμα τοῦ κυρίου ἡμῶν Ἰησοῦ Χριστοῦ τῷ Ἰωσήφ. ὁμοίως δὲ καὶ Δαβὶδ περὶ τῆς ταφῆς αὐτοῦ λέγει ἐν τῷ πζ΄ ψαλμῷ, ὡς ἐκ προσώπου Χριστοῦ, "ἔθεντό με ἐν λάκκῳ κατωτάτῳ ἐν σκοτεινοῖς καὶ ἐν σκιᾷ θανάτου·" ⁱⁱⁱ καὶ πάλιν "καὶ ἐγενήθην ὡσεὶ ἄνθρωπος ἀβοήθητος ἐν νεκροῖς ἐλεύθερος," ᵐᵐᵐ ἢ γοῦν ἀναμάρτητος. γέγραπται δὲ καὶ ἐν τῷ Ἰὼβ οὕτως, "ἀνοίγωνταί σοι φόβῳ πύλαι θανάτου, πυλωροὶ δὲ ᾅδου ἰδόντες σε ἔπτηξαν," ⁿⁿⁿ δῆλον ὅτι αἱ ἐναντίαι τῶν δαιμόνων δυνάμεις. ὁμοίως δὲ καὶ ἐν τῷ ξζ΄ ψαλμῷ οὕτως γέγραπται, "ἐξάγων πεπεδημένους ἐν ἀνδρίᾳ, ὁμοίως τοὺς παραπικραίνοντας τοὺς κατοικοῦντας ἐν τάφοις." ᵒᵒᵒ ὅτι δὲ ὁ χριστὸς ἐν τῷ ᾅδῃ ἀπομένειν οὐκ ἔμελλεν ἀλλὰ τριήμερος ἀνίστασθαι, ψαλμοῦ ιε΄ ἀκούσομεν λέγοντος ὅτι "οὐκ ἐγκαταλείψεις τὴν ψυχήν μου εἰς ᾅδην, οὐδὲ δώσεις τὸν ὅσιόν σου ἰδεῖν διαφθοράν." ᵖᵖᵖ καὶ ὁ προφήτης δὲ Ὡσηὲ οὕτως ἔφη, "πορευθῶμεν καὶ ἐπιστρέψωμεν πρὸς κύριον τὸν θεὸν ἡμῶν, ὅτι αὐτὸς πέπαικεν ἡμᾶς καὶ ἰάσεται ἡμᾶς μετὰ δύο ἡμέρας· καὶ ἐν τῇ τρίτῃ ἡμέρᾳ ἀναστησόμεθα καὶ ζησόμεθα·" qqq ἰδοὺ περὶ τῆς ἀναστάσεως. περὶ δὲ τῶν μυροφόρων γυναικῶν Ἡσαΐας ὁ προφήτης εἶπεν "γυναῖκες ἐρχόμεναι ἀπὸ θέας δεῦτε· οὐ γὰρ λαός ἐστιν ἔχων σύνεσιν." ʳʳʳ περὶ δὲ τῆς ἀναλήψεως Χριστοῦ ἐν ιζ΄ ψαλμῷ γέγραπται "καὶ ἐπέβη ἐπὶ χερουβὶμ, καὶ ἐπετάσθη ἐπὶ πτερύγων ἀνέμων." ˢˢˢ καὶ πάλιν ἐν μζ΄ ψαλμῷ "ἀνέβη ὁ θεὸς ἐν ἀλαλαγμῷ, κύριος ἐν φωνῇ σάλπιγγος." ᵗᵗᵗ καὶ ἐν τῷ προφήτῃ Ζαχαρίᾳ γέγραπται "ἐν τῇ ἡμέρᾳ ἐκείνῃ στήσονται οἱ πόδες κυρίου εἰς τὸ ὄρος τῶν ἐλαιῶν τὸ κατέναντι Ἱερουσαλὴμ ἐξ ἀνατολῶν ἡλίου." ᵘᵘᵘ]

13. Τίς λοιπὸν ἐκ τῶν προφητῶν ταῦτα ἀκούων περὶ Χριστοῦ,[1] οὐχ ὁμολογεῖ αὐτὸν θεὸν ἀληθινόν;

---

[1] τίς λοιπὸν ἐκ τῶν κ.τ.λ. V, τίς τῶν περὶ αὐτοῦ ῥηθέντων P, λοιοῦν ταῦτα πάντα ἀκούων ἐκ τῶν πὸν τίς ταῦτα ἀκούων ἐκ τῶν προθείων προφητῶν περὶ Χριστοῦ, καὶ φητῶν περὶ τοῦ χριστοῦ Ap.

ⁱⁱⁱ Psa. lxxxvii. 7.   ᵐᵐᵐ Psa. lxxxvii. 5-6.   ⁿⁿⁿ Job xxxviii. 17.   ᵒᵒᵒ Psa. lxvii. 7.
ᵖᵖᵖ Psa. xv. 10.   qqq Hos. vi 1-2.   ʳʳʳ Isa. xxvii. 11.   ˢˢˢ Psa. xvii. 11.
ᵗᵗᵗ Psa. xlvi. 6.   ᵘᵘᵘ Zech. xiv. 4.

ἡμεῖς γὰρ οὐκ ἄνθρωπον ψιλὸν αὐτὸν λέγομεν, ἀλλὰ θεὸν ἐνανθρωπήσαντα, καὶ εἴδωλα καταργήσαντα, θυσίας δαιμονικὰς παύσαντα, βωμοὺς καταστρέψαντα. ποῦ εἰσὶν αἱ θυσίαι Αἰγύπτου; ποῦ αἱ μαν-
5 τεῖαι Μέμφεως; ποῦ εἰσὶ σήμερον οἱ τὸν Νεῖλον σεβόμενοι; ποῦ τῆς Ἀρτέμιδος ὁ ναός; ποῦ τοῦ ναοῦ Κυζίκου αἱ μαντεῖαι καὶ θυσίαι; ἀπώλοντο πάντα τὰ τῶν δαιμόνων πράγματα τοῦ Χριστοῦ φανέντος, σταυροῦ παγέντος. Χριστὸς πανταχοῦ προσκυνεῖ-
10 ται καὶ δοξάζεται, καὶ οὐκ αἰσχύνονται οἱ Ἰουδαῖοι εἰδωλοθύτας ἡμᾶς καὶ εἰδωλολάτρας ὀνομάζοντες. ὅμως οὐδὲν ξένον· πᾶσα γὰρ γυνὴ πόρνη τὸ ἴδιον ὄνομα τῇ ἐλευθέρᾳ γυναικὶ περιτίθησιν, κράζουσα πόρνην. Ἡσαΐου καὶ Ἱερεμίου καὶ αὐτοῦ τοῦ δεσπότου οὐκ
15 ἐφείσασθε, καὶ πῶς ἡμῶν ἔχετε φείσασθαι; ἐγὼ μὲν προσκυνῶν εἰκόνα λέγω δόξα σοι ὁ θεὸς τῶν ἁγίων, καὶ οὐ λέγω δόξα σοι ξύλον ἢ ζωγραφία· σὺ δὲ προσκυνῶν τὴν εἰκόνα, λέγεις δόξα σοι Ναβουχοδονόσορ. ἐγὼ προσκυνῶν τὸν σταυρὸν, οὐ
20 λέγω δόξα σοι ξύλον· μὴ γένοιτο· ἀλλὰ λέγω δόξα

² αὐτὸν ψιλὸν P.
³ ἀλλὰ καὶ P.
⁴ ἡμεῖς γὰρ οὐκ κ.τ.λ...... θεὸν om. An.
⁵ καὶ om. PAn.
⁶ εἴδωλά τε An.
⁷ δαιμόνων An.
⁸ παύσαντα, βωμοὺς om. An.
⁹ ποῦ Σεβέννυτος ἢ τὸν Σίμωνα σεβομένη; ποῦ Ὄνουφις ἢ τὸν ὄνον προσκυνοῦσα; διὰ γὰρ τοῦτο τὰ τοιαῦτα ὀνόματα add. P, ποῦ Σεβήννυτος ἢ τὸν Σίμωνα σεβομένη; ποῦ Νοῦφις ἢ τὸν οἶνον προσκυνοῦσα add. An.
¹⁰ ἥλιον An.
¹¹ ναοῦ Κυζίκου VAn., Κυζίκου ναοῦ P.
¹² αἱ θυσίαι P.
¹³ ὅλα P.
¹⁴ αἱ μαντεῖαι καὶ κ.τ.λ. ..... τοῦ Χριστοῦ VP, αἱ μαντεῖαι Ἀπόλ-

λωνος καὶ πάντων τῶν δαιμόνων; τοῦ γὰρ Χριστοῦ An.
¹⁵ καὶ σταυροῦ PAn.
¹⁶ ὁ θεὸς An.
¹⁷ οἱ om. PAn.
¹⁸ καὶ εἰδωλολάτρας ἡμᾶς P.
¹⁹ περιτίθη P.
²⁰ πόρνη P, πεπορνευμένη An.
²¹ πλὴν Ἡσαΐου P.
²² ἡμῶν ἔχετε V, ἔχετε ἡμῶν P, ἡμῖν τοῖς χριστιανοῖς ἔχετε An.
²³ καὶ ἐγὼ P, κἀγὼ An.
²⁴ τὴν εἰκόνα P.
²⁵ ξύλου ἢ ζωγραφίας An.
²⁶ καὶ Au.
²⁷ προσεκύνησας An.
²⁸ εἶπας An.
²⁹ σοι om. An.
³⁰ προσκυνῶ An.
³¹ σοι om. An.
³² ξύλου An. ἢ ζωγραφία σὺ δὲ κ.τ.λ. ...... σοι ξύλον om. P.

σοι σταυρὲ παντοδύναμε ὁ τύπος³³ τοῦ Χριστοῦ·³⁴ σὺ
δὲ προσκυνῶν τὸν μόσχον λέγεις³⁵ "οὗτοι οἱ θεοί σου
Ἰσραὴλ οἱ ἐξαγαγόντες σε ἐκ γῆς Αἰγύπτου."ᵃ ἐγὼ
αἰχμαλωτιζόμενος καὶ τυπτόμενος καὶ σφαζόμενος³⁶
καὶ³⁷ πολλὰ³⁸ καταπονούμενος, τὸν θεόν μου οὐκ ἀρ-
νοῦμαι· εἰ δέ³⁹ τινες χριστιανοὶ⁴⁰ ἠρνήσαντο, ἀλλ'
οὐ τοσοῦτοι⁴¹ ὑμεῖς¹² δὲ μὴ⁴³ φονευθέντες⁴⁴ ἀπὸ ψιλοῦ⁴⁵
τὸν θεὸν πράγματος⁴⁶ ἠρνήσασθε.

14. Καὶ ἐπειδὴ εἴπατε διὰ τί οὐκ εἶπον γυμνῶς οἱ
προφῆται περὶ Χριστοῦ,¹ ἐρωτῶ ὑμᾶς κἀγώ, διὰ τί οὐ
προεῖπον ὑμῖν περὶ τοῦ χριστοῦ,² ὅτι βλέπετε,³ ἐλθεῖν
μέλλει⁴ ἄνθρωπος καλούμενος Ἰησοῦς,⁵ μὴ πιστεύσητε⁶
αὐτῷ ὅτι πλάνος ἐστιν;⁷ ὄντως ἀνόητοι καὶ βραδεῖς
τῇ καρδίᾳ πλάνον καὶ οὐ Χριστὸν⁸ προσδεχόμενοι⁹
ἐστέ.¹⁰

15. Καὶ μηδέν¹ μοι εἴπῃς λοιπὸν μηδὲ ἐγκαλέσῃς²
διὰ τί³ τὰς εἰκόνας⁴ προσκυνῶ. ἀλλ' ἐκεῖνό μοι εἰπὲ
διὰ τί⁵ τὴν εἰκόνα τοῦ Ναβουχοδονόσορ ἐν Βαβυλῶνι
σὺ⁶ προσεκύνησας καίτοι γε ἔχων ἐκεῖ τὸν⁷ Δανιὴλ

---

³³ ὁ τύπος τοῦ σταυροῦ P.
³⁴ ἀλλὰ λέγω δόξα..... τοῦ Χριστοῦ om. An.
³⁵ ἔλεγες P.
³⁶ ἀφαζόμενος P (sic).
³⁷ καὶ τυπτόμενος καὶ σφαζόμενος καὶ om. An.
³⁸ ἔτη πολλὰ P, πολλὰ ἔτη καὶ An.
³⁹ δὲ καί PAn.
⁴⁰ χριστιανοὶ om. P.
⁴¹ οὐ τοσοῦτοι V, οὐ τοσοῦτοι ὡς An., οὕτως οὐκ ἠρνήσαντο ὡς P.
⁴² ἐν Βαβυλῶνι, μήτε τυφθέντες μήτε add. PAn.
⁴³ δὲ μὴ om. PAn.
⁴⁴ δαρέντες τυφθέντες μήτε δαρέντες An.
⁴⁵ ἀλλ' ἀπὸ ψιλοῦ ῥήματος πάντες PAn.
⁴⁶ πράγματος om. P, τὸν θεὸν πράγματος om. An.
¹ τοῦ χριστοῦ PAn.

² καὶ θεοῦ ἡμῶν add. P.
³ βλέπετε om. P.
⁴ ἔχει PAn.
⁵ ὁρᾶτε add P.
⁶ πιστεύσειτε P, πιστεύσατε An.
⁷ καὶ ὅσα ὑμεῖς κατ' αὐτοῦ ἐξ-
αγών κακίστου διανοίας καὶ ἀναισ-
χυντίας καὶ παραπληξίας λέγετε
add. P. ἀλλ' οὕτως τὸν ἀληθινὸν
Χριστὸν καὶ θεόν, ὅν οἱ προφῆται
προεκήρυξαν, καὶ θελήσαντες,
πλάνον καὶ οὐ Χριστὸν ἐκδέχεσθε
add. An.
⁸ ἔσεσθαι add. P.
⁹ προσδεδεγμένοι P.
¹⁰ ἐστέ om. P.   ¹ μὴ P.
² μηδὲ ἐγκαλέσῃς om. P.
³ ἐγὼ add. P.
⁴ τὴν εἰκόνα τοῦ Χριστοῦ P.
⁵ σύ add. P.
⁶ σύ om. P.
⁷ τὸν om. P.

ᵃ Ex. xxxii. 4.

καὶ Ἱερεμίαν καὶ Ἰεζεκιὴλ [8] καὶ ἄλλους προφήτας διδάσκοντάς σε; καὶ εἰκόνι προσεκυνήσατε ἀνθρώπου,[9] καὶ εἰ μὴ[10] οἱ τρεῖς παῖδες καὶ[11] μόνοι[12] πιστὰ[13] τῷ θεῷ[14] ἐφύλαξαν,[15] καίτοι γε τοσαῦτα σημεῖα καὶ τέρατα
5 θεωρήσαντες[16] ἐν Αἰγύπτῳ καὶ ἐν παντὶ τόπῳ ὑπὸ Μωϋσέως[17] ἐν τῇ ἐρυθρᾷ θαλάσσῃ,[18] ἐν τῇ ἐρήμῳ, ἐν τῷ ὄρει τῷ Σινά,[19] ἐν στύλῳ πυρὸς, ἐν νεφέλῃ φωτός.[20] πότε ὁ θεὸς τοιαῦτα ἐποίησε τινί;[21] πότε ὁ θεός τινι ἐλάλησεν ἐν Σινά[22] οὕτως[23] διὰ νόμου, καὶ σαλπίγ-
10 γων,[24] καὶ πυρός, καὶ φωνῶν, καὶ σημείων τοιούτων, νόμον δοὺς ὑμῖν,[25] μάννα βρέξας, προφήτας ἀναδείξας, τὰ ἔθνη ὑποτάξας, ἀλλοφύλους[26] ἐξολοθρεύσας, τὰς πλάκας ἐπιδούς,[27] τὴν σκηνὴν ὑμῶν αὐτὸς διατυπώσας, Μωϋσέα[28] ὡς[29] δεύτερον θεὸν τοποποιὸν[30] ὑμῖν[31]
15 καταστήσας; ὦ τῆς πολλῆς ὑμῶν πωρώσεως· ὦ τῆς κακῆς[32] ὑμῶν γνώμης· ὦ τῆς ἀχαρίστου ὑμῶν προαιρέσεως καὶ τυφλώσεως· ἄνω ἐν τῷ ὄρει Μωϋσῆς[33] ὑπὲρ ὑμῶν ἠγωνίζετο[34] καὶ κάτω ὑμεῖς τὸν μόσχον ἐχωνεύετε· ἄνω ἐκεῖνος τὸν θεὸν παρεκάλει καὶ[35] σὺ τὸν μόσχον
20 προσεκύνεις· τὸ μάννα ἤσθιες καὶ τὸν θεὸν ὕβριζες· λέγει γὰρ ὁ Δαβὶδ[36] "ἔτι τῆς βρώσεως οὔσης ἐν τῷ στόματι αὐτῶν καὶ ὀργὴ[37] τοῦ θεοῦ ἀνέβη ἐπ᾽ αὐ-

---

[8] Ἰεζεκιὴλ P, Ἐζεκίαν V. καὶ Ἱερεμίαν καὶ Ἰεζεκιὴλ om. An.
[9] ἀνθρώπου προσεκυνήσατε P.
[10] καὶ εἰ μὴ VAn., εἰ καὶ P.
[11] καὶ om. P. [12] καὶ μόνοι om. An.
[13] τὰ πιστὰ P. [14] τῷ θεῷ om. P.
[15] ποῦ ὑμεῖς τῷ θεῷ πιστὰ ἐφυλάξατε; add. P. ποῦ εἰπέ μοι πιστὰ ἐφυλάξατε τῷ θεῷ; add. An.
[16] θεωρήσαντες VAn., θεωρήσας V.
[17] Μωσέως PV.
[18] ἐν τῇ θαλάσσῃ τῇ ἐρυθρᾷ P.
[19] τῷ Σινά om. P, ἐν τῷ ὄρει τῷ Σινά om. An.
[20] ἐν τῷ ὄρει Σινά add. PAn.
[21] πότε ὁ θεὸς τοιαῦτα ἀγαθὰ ἐποίησε, πότε τινί; P. πότε ὁ θεὸς τοιαῦτα ἀγαθά τινι ἐποίησεν; An.

[22] ἐν Σινά om. PAn.
[23] οὕτω P.
[24] ἀγγελικῶν add. PAn.
[25] ὑμῖν PAn., ἡμῖν V.
[26] ἀλλοφύλους PAn., ἀλλοφύλους V.
[27] ἐπιδεδωκὼς V, ἐπιδώσας An.
[28] Μωσέα PV.
[29] ὡς om. An.
[30] τοποποιοῦντα PAn.
[31] ὑμῖν P, αὐτοῦ πρὸς ὑμᾶς P, αὐτὸν πρὸς ὑμᾶς An.
[32] κακίστης P.
[33] Μωσῆς V.
[34] ἠγωνίζητο V.
[35] κάτω add. PAn.
[36] ὅτι add. An., καὶ τοῦ Δαβὶδ ἄκουσον λέγοντος pro λέγει γὰρ ὁ Δαβὶδ P.
[37] ἡ ὀργὴ P.

τοὺς·" ᵃ ³⁸ καὶ ³⁹ μή μοι εἴπῃς ⁴⁰ διὰ τί τὸν ⁴¹ υἱὸν τοῦ ⁴²
Θεοῦ προσκυνῶ· ἀλλ' εἰπέ μοι σὺ,⁴³ διὰ τί' ὑμεῖς υἱοὺς ⁴⁴
καὶ θυγατέρας ὑμῶν,⁴⁵ ὡς λέγει Δαβὶδ, ἐθύσατε τοῖς
δαιμονίοις,⁴⁶ καὶ ⁴⁷ τῷ ⁴⁸ Βεελφεγώρ; μὴ γὰρ ὑμεῖς πίστιν ἔχετε· μὴ γένοιτο. ἄκουσον ⁴⁹ Μωϋσέως ⁵⁰ πρὸς τὸν 5
λαὸν λέγοντος,⁵¹ καίτοι γε τότε φησὶ⁵² θεοσεβὴς ἦν ὁ
λαὸς τῶν Ἑβραίων—ἀλλ' ἄκουσον τί λέγει Μωϋσῆς,⁵³
" γενεὰ ἐξεστραμμένη ⁵⁴ ἐστίν, υἱοὶ ⁵⁵ οἷς οὐκ ἔστι πίστις
ἐν αὐτοῖς·"ᵇ καὶ πάλιν " οὗτος ὁ λαὸς μωρὸς καὶ οὐχὶ
σοφός·"ᶜ καὶ πάλιν " γενεὰ σκολιὰ καὶ διεστραμμένη, 10
ταῦτα κυρίῳ ἀνταποδίδοτε."ᵈ καὶ ἄλλα μυρία περὶ
ὑμῶν ⁵⁶ ἐν τοῖς προφήταις ⁵⁷ ἐκ θεοῦ ⁵⁸ εἴρηνται·" ⁵⁹ "υἱοὺς"
γὰρ φησὶν " ἐγέννησα καὶ ὕψωσα, αὐτοὶ δέ με ἠθέτη-
σαν. καὶ⁶⁰ ἔγνω βοῦς τὸν κτησάμενον καὶ ὄνος τὴν
φάτνην τοῦ κυρίου αὐτοῦ· Ἰσραὴλ δέ⁶¹ με οὐκ ἔγνω 15
καὶ ὁ λαός με οὐ συνῆκεν. οὐαὶ ἔθνος ἁμαρτωλὸν,
λαὸς πλήρης ἀνομιῶν."⁶² ᵉ καὶ πάλιν ὁ αὐτὸς προφήτης
Ἡσαΐας πρὸς ὑμᾶς φησὶν ⁶³ " ἀκούσατε λόγον κυρίου,

³⁸ καὶ πάλιν ἐν πᾶσιν τούτοις
ἥμαρτον ἔτι λέγοντες "ἐπεὶ ἐπά-
ταξε πέτραν, καὶ ἐρρύησαν ὕδατα,
καὶ χείμαρροι κατεκλύσθησαν· μὴ
καὶ ἄρτον δύναται δοῦναι, ἢ ἑτοι-
μάσαι τράπεζαν τῷ λαῷ αὐτοῦ;"ᶠ
οὐ διὰ τοῦτο λέγει ὅτι "ἤκουσε
κύριος καὶ ἀνεβάλετο, καὶ πῦρ
ἀνήφθη ἐν Ἰακώβ, καὶ ὀργὴ ἀνέβη
ἐπὶ τὸν Ἰσραήλ";ᵍ add. P.
³⁹ καὶ cm. P.   ⁴⁰ οὖν λοιπὸν ad. P.
⁴¹ τὸν om. P.   ⁴² τοῦ om. P.
⁴³ σὺ om. P.
⁴⁴ τοὺς υἱοὺς P.
⁴⁵ ὑμῶν καὶ τὰς θυγατέρας PAn.
⁴⁶ ὡς λέγει Δαβὶδ, ἐθύσατε τοῖς
δαιμονίοις, VAn., ἐθύσατε τοῖς δαιμονίοις, ὡς λέγει ὁ Δαβὶδ P.
⁴⁷ ἔθυσαν add. P.
⁴⁸ γλυπτῷ add. P.
⁴⁹ καὶ ἄκουσον P.   ⁵⁰ Μωσέως V.
⁵¹ λέγοντος πρὸς τὸν λαὸν PAn.
⁵² φησὶ om. PAn.

⁵³ θεοσεβὴς ἦν ὁ λαὸς κ.τ.λ. ....
Μωϋσῆς VAn., πρὸς καιρὸν θεο-
σεβοῦντος τοῦ λαοῦ, ἀλλ' ὅμως τὴν
εἰς ὕστερον ὑμῶν ἀσέβειαν προλέ-
γοντος καὶ ἐλέγχοντος καὶ P.
⁵⁴ γενεὰν ἐξεστραμμένην P.
⁵⁵ ἐστιν, υἱοὶ om. P. υἱοὶ om. et εἰσὶν
pro ἐστιν An. ἀποκαλοῦντος καὶ ἐν
add. P.
⁵⁶ ἄλλαι μυρίαι μαρτυρίαι πονηραὶ περὶ ὑμῶν εἰσὶν P, ἄλλαι μυρίαι μαρτυρίαι περὶ ὑμῶν πονηραὶ
εἰσὶν An.
⁵⁷ ἐν ταῖς προφητικαῖς βίβλοις P,
ἐν ταῖς προφητείαις ὑμῶν An.
⁵⁸ τοῦ θεοῦ PAn.
⁵⁹ εἰρημέναι PAn.
⁶⁰ καὶ om. PAn.   ⁶¹ μου PAn.
⁶² ἁμαρτιῶν PAn.
⁶³ φησὶν om. An. Ἡσαΐας πρὸς
ὑμᾶς φησὶν om. et ἁμαρτίας ὑμῶν
ἐκκαλύπτων πονηρὰς οὕτω στη-
λιτεύων λέγει add. P.

ᵃ Psa. lxxvii. 30-31.   ᵇ Deut. xxxii. 20.   ᶜ Ibid. vers. 6.   ᵈ Ibid. 5-6.
ᵉ Isa. i. 2-4.   ᶠ Psa. lxxvii. 20.   ᵍ Ibid. vers. 21.

ἄρχοντες Σοδόμων· προσέχετε λόγον [64] κυρίου, λαὸς
Γομόρρας."[h] ὁρᾶτε ὅτι Σοδομίτας καὶ ἀπίστους, καὶ
λαὸν μωρὸν λέγει τοὺς Ἰουδαίους[65] ὁ θεὸς, καὶ εἰδωλοθύτας, καὶ τεκνοθύτας, καὶ εἰκονολάτρας, καὶ ἀπίστους,
5 καὶ[66] ἀχαρίστους,[67] καὶ ἐσκοτισμένους, καὶ ἀγνώμονας,[68]
καὶ γενεὰν πονηρὰν καὶ διεστραμμένην, καὶ τέκνα μω-
μητά·[69] "καὶ ἔθυσαν[70] δαιμονίοις καὶ οὐ θεῷ·"[i] "καὶ ἐγ-
κατέλιπον[71] θεὸν τὸν ποιήσαντα αὐτοὺς, καὶ ἀπέστησαν[72]
ἀπὸ θεοῦ σωτῆρος αὐτῶν."[k] [73] ἐρευνήσωμεν οὖν καὶ[74]
10 τὰς γραφὰς,[75] ἐὰν[76] περὶ ἄλλου οἱουδήποτε ἔθνους ἢ
γένους[77] τοιαῦτα καὶ[78] τοσαῦτα κακὰ[79] ὁ θεὸς κατήγ-
γειλεν, ἢ ἐμαρτύρησε δικαίως.[80]

16. Καὶ γὰρ ἐν Ἱεροσολύμοις πεντήκοντα καὶ[1] δύο
ἔτη ἐποίησαν θύοντες ἐν τῷ ναῷ[2] τοῖς εἰδώλοις[3] καὶ τῷ
15 διαβόλῳ ἐπὶ Μανασσῇ τοῦ βασιλέως βεβηλωσάντες τὸν
ναὸν καὶ τὴν πόλιν τοῦ θεοῦ.[4] διὰ τοῦτο ἐν Βαβυλῶνι
καὶ ἅπαξ καὶ δεύτερον παρέδωκεν ὑμᾶς[5] τοῖς Χαλδαίοις
εἰς αἰχμαλωσίαν· εἶτα πάλιν ὑμᾶς μετὰ ἑβδομήκοντα[6]
ἔτη ἀνεκαλέσατο. ἄρτι οὖν θέλω μαθεῖν ἐξ[7] ὑμῶν
20 μετὰ τὸ ἀνελθεῖν ὑμᾶς ἐκ Βαβυλῶνος καὶ κτισθῆναι
τὸν ναὸν ὑμῶν ἐκ δευτέρου[8] ἐν Ἱεροσολύμοις καὶ ἐν
αὐτῷ ὑμᾶς προσκυνεῖν τῷ θεῷ καὶ οὐχὶ εἰδώλοις[9] ποίαν
ἁμαρτίαν ἐποιήσατε ἐνώπιον τοῦ θεοῦ; ὅτι ἰδοὺ ἑξακόσια[10] ἔτη[11] ἐν πάσῃ τῇ γῇ ἐσκόρπισεν ὑμᾶς,[12] καὶ
25 ἤγαγε Τῖτον καὶ Οὐεσπασιανὸν ἀπὸ Ῥώμης, καὶ διέφ-

[64] νόμον PAn.
[65] τοὺς Ἰουδαίους λέγει pro λέγει τοὺς Ἰουδαίους PAn.
[66] καὶ om. P.   [67] τε add P.
[68] τε υἱοὺς add. P.
[69] ἵππους τε θηλυμανεῖς add. P.
[70] θύοντας P.
[71] ἐγκαταλιπόντας P.
[72] ἀποστάντας P.   [73] αὐτοῦ P.
[74] οὖν καὶ V, δὴ P, οὖν An.
[75] λοιπὸν add. An.   [76] εἴπερ P.
[77] ἢ γένους om. PAn.
[78] τοιαῦτα καὶ om. An.
[79] κακὰ om. An.
[80] ἐνδίκως P. ἢ ἐμαρτύρησε δικαίως om. An.

[1] καὶ om. PAn.
[2] τοῦ θεοῦ add. PAn.
[3] τοῖς δαίμοσιν P.
[4] τοῦ θεοῦ καὶ τὴν πόλιν P.
[5] ὁ θεὸς add. PAn.
[6] οἱ P.
[7] παρ' P.
[8] ἐκ δευτέρου τὸν ναὸν ὑμῶν PAn.
[9] οὐ τοῖς εἰδώλοις P, οὐκέτι τοῖς εἰδώλοις An.
[10] ἑξακόσια om. P. ὀκτακόσια καὶ πλείονα pro ἑξακόσια An.
[11] χίλια add. P.
[12] ἐσκόρπισεν ὑμᾶς ἐν πάσῃ τῇ γῇ P.

[h] Isa. i. 10.   [i] Deut. xxxii. 17.   [k] Ibid. 15.

θειρε[13] καὶ ἔσφαξεν[14] ἐν Ἱερουσαλὴμ περί που[15] ἑκατὸν καὶ δέκα μυριάδας[16] ὡς Ἰώσηπος[17] συνεγράψατο· καὶ ἐνεπύρισαν τὸν ναὸν, καὶ ἐρήμωσαν τὸ θυσιαστήριον, καὶ τὰ ἅγια, καὶ τὴν πόλιν πᾶσαν, καὶ τὴν Σιὼν, καὶ ᾐχμαλώτευσαν[18] ὑμᾶς· καὶ ἔστε ἐν πάσῃ τῇ γῇ διεσ- 5 παρμένοι καὶ[19] παρανομοῦντες ἕως τῆς σήμερον. καὶ ἰδοὺ ἑξακόσια ἑβδομήκοντα[20] ἔτη οὐ θυσιαστήριον, οὐ κιβωτὸς, οὐ προφήτης, οὐ τόπος, οὐ τοῦ[21] πάσχα φυλακή.[22] εἶπε γὰρ[23] ὑμῖν ὁ θεὸς μηδαμοῦ[24] ποιῆσαι τὸ πάσχα ἔξω Ἱεροσολύμων, μήτε ἐν Αἰγύπτῳ εἰσελθεῖν.[25] ἰδοὺ[26] οἱ 10 πατέρες ὑμῶν ἁμαρτήσαντες ἀπέλαβον[27] δεύτερον αἰχμαλωτισθέντες, καὶ ὁ ναὸς δὲ ἠρημώθη, καὶ διηλλάγη ὑμῖν ὁ θεός·[28] νῦν[29] δὲ ποίαν ἁμαρτίαν ἐποιήσατε, καὶ τοιαύτην μεγάλην, ὅτι οὐκέτι ἤγειρεν[30] ὑμῖν[31] τὸν ναὸν, οὐκέτι[32] ἀνήγαγεν ὑμᾶς ἐκ τῶν ἐθνῶν ;[33] ἆρα[34] εἰδώλοις ἐθύσα- 15 τε[35] τοὺς υἱοὺς καὶ τὰς θυγατέρας ὑμῶν[36] ὥσπερ[37] οἱ πατέρες ὑμῶν ; ἆρα εἰκόνι προσεκυνήσατε ὡς ἐκεῖνοι ; ἆρα εἰς τὸν ναὸν εἴδωλον ἐστήσατε ὥσπερ[38] ὁ[39] Μανασσῆς ;

---

[13] διέφθειρε om. An. ἐρήμωσαν P.
[14] ἔσφαξαν ἐξ ὑμῶν PAn.
[15] περί που om. P. pro eodem κἂν An.
[16] ἑκατὸν καὶ δέκα μυριάδας V, μυριάδας ρί P, ἑκατὸν μυριάδας An.
[17] Ἰώσηπος ὁ ὑμῶν συγγραφεὺς μόνος ταῦτα ἐκθέμενος An., Ἰώσηππος ὁ σοφὸς ὑμῶν συγγραφεὺς P.
[18] ᾐχμαλώτησαν P (sic).
[19] καὶ om. P.
[20] ἑξακόσια ἑβδομήκοντα V, λοιπὸν χίλια P, ὀκτακόσια καὶ πλείονα An. [21] τοῦ om. P.
[22] φυλάττοντες P.
[23] εἶπε γὰρ V, καὶ γὰρ εἶπεν P.
[24] μηδαμῶς ἀλλαχοῦ P.
[25] ἔξω κ.τ.λ.... εἰσελθεῖν V, εἰ μὴ ἐν Ἱερουσαλήμ P, εἰ μὴ ἐν Ἱερουσαλήμ· μηδὲ εἰς Αἴγυπτον εἰσελθεῖν An. [26] καὶ ἰδοὺ λοιπὸν P.
[27] ἀπέλαβον An., ἀπέλανον V, om. P.

[28] δεύτερον αἰχμαλωτισθέντες κ.τ.λ.... ὑμῖν ὁ θεός V, δεύτερον ἐν Βαβυλῶνι αἰχμαλωτευθέντες ἐκ δευτέρου, καὶ δευτέρου τοῦ ναοῦ ἐρημωθέντος, καὶ διαλλαγῆναι αὐτοὺς τὸν θεὸν καὶ οἰκοδομηθῆναι τὸν ναόν An., ἐν Αἰγύπτῳ πρότερον, εἶτα εἰς Βαβυλῶνα ἀπῆλθον αἰχμαλωτισθέντες, καὶ τὴν πόλιν πάλιν ἀπέλαβον καταλλαγέντος ὑμῖν τοῦ θεοῦ, καὶ ᾠκοδομήθη ὁ ναός P.
[29] νῦν δὲ V, ὑμεῖς δὲ P, ὑμεῖς καὶ An. [30] ἀνήγειρεν P.
[31] ὑμῖν om. P.
[32] οὐκέτι VAn., ὑμῶν, οὔτε P.
[33] ὑμᾶς ἐκ τῶν ἐθνῶν συνήγαγεν; P. ἀνήγαγεν ὑμᾶς ἐκ τῶν ἐχθρῶν ; An.
[34] ὑμεῖς add. P.
[35] ὑμεῖς add. An.
[36] τοῖς δαιμονίοις add. P.
[37] ὡς PAn.
[38] ὡς PAn.
[39] ὁ om. P.

ἆρα προφήτας ἀπεκτείνατε; οὐδαμῶς.⁴⁰ τίνος οὖν ἕνεκεν οὕτως ὑπὸ θεοῦ⁴¹ ἐγκατελείφθητε; ἀληθῶς κἂν ὑμεῖς μὴ εἴπητε τὴν αἰτίαν, κἂν ὑμεῖς σιγήσητε, οἱ λίθοι κεκράξονται, ὅτι ἀφ' οὗ τὸν Χριστὸν ἐσταυρώσατε
5 μέχρι καὶ νῦν καὶ εἰς τὸν αἰῶνα διεσκορπίσθητε,⁴² ἐγυμνώθητε,⁴² ἐδιώχθητε, τοῦ ναοῦ καὶ τῆς Σιὼν⁴³ καὶ πάσης τῆς⁴⁴ τοῦ νόμου λατρείας.⁴⁵ οἱ γὰρ πατέρες ὑμῶν οἱ⁴⁶ μοσχοποιήσαντες,⁴⁷ καὶ ἐν τῷ ναῷ τοῦ θεοῦ ἁμαρτήσαντες,⁴⁸ καὶ τοὺς υἱοὺς αὐτῶν καὶ τὰς θυγατέρας⁴⁹ τοῖς
10 δαιμονίοις⁵⁰ θύσαντες, ἑβδομήκοντα ἔτη καὶ ἑκατὸν⁵¹ ἐν Βαβυλῶνι τῆς Περσίδος παιδευθέντες, συνεχωρήθησαν πάντα⁵² ἐκεῖνα τὰ ἁμαρτήματα,⁵³ καὶ ἀνεκλήθησαν·⁵⁴ ὑμεῖς δὲ οἱ⁵⁵ εἰς Χριστὸν⁵⁶ ἁμαρτήσαντες οὐχὶ⁵⁷ ἑβδομήκοντα ἔτη ἢ ἑκατὸν ἐν Βαβυλῶνι τῆς Περσίδος
15 ἐπαιδεύθητε,⁵⁸ ἀλλ' ἕως τῆς συντελείας τοῦ αἰῶνος ἐξεβλήθητε· ἡμεῖς δὲ τὰ ἔθνη ὑπὸ⁵⁹ Χριστοῦ ἐκλήθημεν, καὶ αὐτῷ δουλεύομεν, καὶ αὐτὸν⁶⁰ δοξάζομεν ἅμα τῷ πατρὶ καὶ⁶¹ τῷ ἁγίῳ⁶² πνεύματι εἰς τοὺς αἰῶνας·⁶³ ἀμήν.⁶⁴

20 [17.¹ Ἵνα δὲ ἐκ πολλῆς περιουσίας, καὶ τὰ τῶν Ἰουδαίων ἀναίσχυντα στόματα καὶ βλάσφημα ἐμφράξω-

⁴⁰ οὐδαμῶς om. et ἆρα μὴ καὶ ὑμεῖς ὡς οἱ πατέρες ὑμῶν τὸν χαλκοῦν ὄφιν, τὸν ὑπὸ τοῦ Μωϋσέως πεποιημένον, προσεκυνήσατε, καὶ ἐσεβάσθητε ὡς οἱ πατέρες ὑμῶν; καὶ γὰρ καὶ τοῦτο εἰς ἔλεγχον ὑμῶν γέγραπται add. P.
⁴¹ τοῦ θεοῦ P.
⁴² καὶ add. P.
⁴³ Σιὼν VAn., πόλεως P.
⁴⁴ πάντων τῶν P.
⁴⁵ λατρειῶν P.
⁴⁶ οἱ VAn., καὶ P.
⁴⁷ καὶ πολλὰ παρανομήσαντες add. P, πολλὰ παρανομήσαντες add. An.
⁴⁸ ἀσεβήσαντες P.
⁴⁹ καὶ τὰς θυγατέρας om. P.
⁵⁰ τῷ διαβόλῳ PAn.
⁵¹ ἑβδομήκοντα ἔτη καὶ ἑκατὸν om. P. VAn., ὁ ἔτη ἢ καὶ πλεῖον P.
⁵² ὅλα P.
⁵³ τὰ ἁμαρτήματα ἐκεῖνα P.
⁵⁴ ἀνεκλήθησαν PAn., ἀνεκλίθησαν V.
⁵⁵ οἱ om. P.
⁵⁶ εἰς τὸν Χριστὸν P, ἐν Χριστῷ An.
⁵⁷ οὐχ PAn.
⁵⁸ ἑβδομήκοντα ἔτη κ.τ.λ. ..... ἐπαιδεύθητε V, ἑβδομήκοντα οὐδὲ ἑκατὸν ἔτη μόνα An., ἑβδομήκοντα ἔτη P.
⁵⁹ υἱοὶ An.
⁶⁰ αὐτῷ An.
⁶¹ σὺν An.
⁶² αὐτοῦ add. An.
⁶³ τῶν αἰώνων add. An.
⁶⁴ ἡμεῖς δὲ τὰ ἔθνη ὑπὸ Χριστοῦ ἐκλήθημεν κ.τ.λ. ..... ἀμὴν om. P.
¹ ad finem P. totum om. V.

μεν, καὶ ἡμῖν τοῖς ὑπὸ Χριστοῦ σεσωσμένοις πλείονα
τὰ νικητήρια ὑπάρξῃ ἀναγκαίως αὐτά. καὶ ἀπὸ τῶν
τοῦ Δανιὴλ λόγων, μᾶλλον δὲ τῶν τοῦ θεοῦ τῶν ὑπὸ
τοῦ ἀγγέλου πρὸς αὐτὸν ῥηθέντων, ποιησώμεθα τὴν
ἐξέτασιν, ἀποδεικνύντες ὅτι λοιπὸν τοῦ θεοῦ τέλεον 5
ἀποστραφέντος τὰ τῶν Ἰουδαίων, οὐκέτι λοιπὸν παρ'
αὐτοῖς οὔτε ἱερωσύνη, οὔτε ναὸς, οὔτε αὐτὰ τὰ τῆς πόλεως ἤδη καὶ πράγματα ἐπανήξει· καὶ δῆλον ἀπ'αὐτῶν
τῶν τοῦ ἀγγέλου ῥημάτων, "Δανιὴλ" γὰρ φησὶν "ἀνὴρ
ἐπιθυμιῶν, σύνες ἐν τοῖς λόγοις οἷς ἐγὼ ἦλθον λαλῆσαι 10
πρός σε, ὅτι εἰς καιροῦ πέρας ὁ ἑβδομάδες, φησὶ, συνετ-
μήθησαν ἐπὶ τὸν λαόν σου, καὶ ἐπὶ τὴν πόλιν τοῦ οἰκο-
δομηθῆναι·"ᵃ "καὶ οἰκοδομηθήσεται πλατεῖα καὶ περί-
τειχος, καὶ ἐκκενωθήσονται οἱ καιροί·"ᵇ καὶ "ἀπὸ
ἐξόδου λόγων τοῦ οἰκοδομηθῆναι Ἱερουσαλὴμ ἕως 15
Χριστοῦ ἡγουμένου ἑβδομάδες ἑπτὰ καὶ ἑβδομάδες
ἑξηκονταδύο,"ᶜ ὅπερ εἰσὶν ἔτη τετρακόσια πγ'· "καὶ
ἀρθήσεται θυσία καὶ σπονδὴ καὶ ἐπὶ τὸ ἱερὸν βδέλυγμα
τῆς ἐρημώσεως."ᵈ πότε οὖν ἤρθη ἡ θυσία, καὶ ἡ σπονδὴ, καὶ ἡ θυσία τοῦ νόμου; οὐχὶ τοῦ χριστοῦ ἐλθόντος; 20
τίς ἐστιν ὁ χρισθεὶς ἅγιος ἁγίων εἰ μὴ ὁ χριστός; περὶ
οὗ καὶ τῆς ἐνδόξου αὐτοῦ παρουσίας λέγει ὁ αὐτὸς Δανιὴλ
"ἐθεώρουν ἐν ὁράματι τῆς νυκτὸς, καὶ ἰδοὺ μετὰ τῶν
νεφελῶν τοῦ οὐρανοῦ ὡς υἱὸς ἀνθρώπου ἐρχόμενος,
καὶ ἕως τοῦ παλαιοῦ τῶν ἡμερῶν ἔφθασεν, καὶ προση- 25
νέχθη αὐτῷ· καὶ αὐτῷ ἐδόθη ἡ ἀρχὴ, καὶ ἡ τιμὴ, καὶ ἡ
βασιλεία, καὶ πάντες οἱ λαοὶ, φυλαὶ, γλῶσσαι αὐτῷ δου-
λεύσουσιν· ἡ ἐξουσία αὐτοῦ ἐξουσία αἰώνιος ἥτις οὐ
παρελεύσεται, καὶ ἡ βασιλεία αὐτοῦ εἰς τοὺς αἰῶνας
οὐ διαφθαρήσεται."ᵉ ἰδοὺ σαφῶς διὰ τῶν εἰρημένων 30
ἐμάθομεν ὅτι αὐτός ἐστιν ὁ υἱὸς τοῦ θεοῦ, ὁ σαρκωθεὶς
καὶ παθὼν δι' ἡμᾶς, καὶ ἀναστὰς ἐκ νεκρῶν, καὶ ἀναλη-
φθεὶς ἐν δόξῃ πρὸς τὸν αὐτοῦ πατέρα, καὶ μέλλων ἔρχεσθαι μετὰ τῶν νεφελῶν τοῦ οὐρανοῦ καὶ δόξης οὐρα-
νίου κρῖναι ζῶντας καὶ νεκρούς. ὅμως καὶ τῶν λοιπῶν 35
ἀκούσωμεν, "ἐθεώρουν" γὰρ φησὶν "ἕως οὗ θρόνοι
ἐτέθησαν, καὶ ὁ παλαιὸς τῶν ἡμερῶν ἐκάθισεν· τὸ
ἔνδυμα αὐτοῦ λευκὸν ὡσεὶ χιὼν, καὶ ἡ θρὶξ τῆς κεφαλῆς
αὐτοῦ ὡσεὶ ἔριον καθαρὸν· ὁ θρόνος αὐτοῦ φλὸξ πυρὸς,

ᵃ Dan. ix. 23-24.   ᵇ Ibid. vers. 25.   ᶜ Ibid.   ᵈ vers. 27   ᵉ Dan. vii. 13-14.

οἱ τροχοὶ αὐτοῦ πῦρ φλέγον· ποταμὸς πυρὸς εἷλκεν ἔμπροσθεν αὐτοῦ· χίλιαι χιλιάδες ἐλειτούργουν αὐτῷ, καὶ μύριαι μυριάδες παρειστήκεισαν αὐτῷ· κριτήριον ἐκάθισεν, καὶ βίβλοι ἠνεῴχθησαν."[f] "ἔφριξεν τὸ πνεῦμά μου, ἐγὼ Δανιήλ."[g] λοιπὸν δεῖ πιστώσασθαι τὰ εἰρημένα ἐκ τῶν τοῦ ἀγγέλου ῥημάτων, ὅτι παρὰ Ἰουδαίοις οὐκέτι ἔσται οὔτε ναός, οὔτε πόλις, οὔτε τι τῶν παρ' αὐτοῖς νομίμων. εἰ καὶ ἐξ ἄκρας ἀνοίας ταῦτα προσδοκῶσιν ἄκουσον οὖν τί ὁ ἄγγελος εἴρηκεν, ὅτι φησὶν "ἕως συντελείας καιρῶν συντέλεια δωθήσεται ἐπὶ τὴν ἐρήμωσιν,"[h] τουτέστιν ἕως συντελείας τῶν αἰώνων καὶ τοῦ κόσμου παντὸς συντέλεια δωθήσεται ἐπὶ τὴν ἐρήμωσιν τῆς τε πόλεως καὶ τοῦ ναοῦ τοῦ ἰουδαϊκοῦ· ἕως, φησὶ, συντελείας καιρῶν καὶ αἰώνων ἐρήμωσις τελείως καθέξει τὰ τῶν Ἰουδαίων· ὅταν δὲ ἀκούσεις, ὦ Ἰουδαῖε, συντέλειαν, τί λοιπὸν προσδοκᾷς; τί νοῦν δεῖ προσέχειν τῷ λέγοντι, ἕως συντελείας συντέλειαν ἔσεσθαι καὶ ἐρήμωσιν, ἢ τοῖς ληρῳδοῦσιν ῥήμασιν ἀναποδείκτοις; ἵνα δὲ μὴ ἐπιμείκιστον καὶ πέρα τῆς διηγήσεως ἐκτείνωμεν τὸν λόγον, ὅπερ μικροῦ δεῖν ἡμᾶς παρέδραμε, τοῦτο προσθέντες τοῖς εἰρημένοις καταπαύσωμεν τὸν λόγον· διὸ φησὶν ὁ λέγων "ἐθεώρουν τότε ἀπὸ φωνῆς τῶν λόγων τῶν μεγάλων ὧν τὸ πέρας ἐκεῖνο ἐλάλει, ἕως ἀνῃρέθη τὸ θηρίον·"[i] πρόδηλον δὲ ὅτι τὸ θηρίον ὁ ἀντίχριστός ἐστιν· ὁ γὰρ υἱὸς τοῦ θεοῦ· "ἐρχόμενος ἐπὶ τῶν νεφελῶν τοῦ οὐρανοῦ,"[k] καθὼς γέγραπται, "ἀνελεῖ αὐτὸν τῷ πνεύματι τοῦ στόματος αὐτοῦ·"[l] αὐτῷ γὰρ πρέπει ἡ δόξα εἰς τοὺς αἰῶνας τῶν αἰώνων. ἀμήν.

18. Ταῦτα ἐκ πολλῶν ὀλίγα ἐκ τῶν ἁγίων προφητῶν παρεθέμεθα πρὸς μὲν ἡμετέραν τῶν χριστιανῶν μείζονα πίστωσιν, πρὸς ἔλεγχον δὲ τῆς ἰουδαϊκῆς σκληροκαρδίας καὶ φρενοβλαβίας, ὅτι ὁ εἷς τῆς ἁγίας καὶ ζωοποιοῦ τριάδος θεὸς, λόγος καὶ θεοῦ υἱὸς, ὁ κύριος ἡμῶν Ἰησοῦς Χριστὸς, αὐτὸς διὰ τὴν ἡμετέραν σωτηρίαν ἐπ' ἐσχάτων τῶν ἡμερῶν ἐνηνθρώπισεν ἐκ τῆς παναγίας ἀχράντου δεσποίνης ἡμῶν θεοτόκου καὶ ἀεὶ παρθένου Μαρίας, καὶ πάντα θεοπρεπῶς ἀπεργασάμενος, καθὼς καὶ οἱ ἅγιοι

---

[f] Ibid. vers. 9-10.   [g] vers. 15.   [h] Dan. ix. 27.   [i] vii. 11.
[k] cf. Dan. vii. 13; Matt. xxiv. 30.   [l] cf. Isa. xi. 4.

προφῆται προεῖπον, ἔσωσεν ἐκ τῆς τοῦ εχθροῦ πλάνης
καὶ δουλείας τὸ γένος ἡμῶν· ὑπὲρ οὖν τῶν τοσούτων
εὐεργεσιῶν, ὧν τυχεῖν παρὰ τῆς αὐτοῦ ἀγαθότητος
ἠξιώθημεν, σπουδάσωμεν αὐτῷ εὐάρεστοι ἀναδειχθῆ-
ναι διὰ τῆς τῶν ἁγίων αὐτοῦ ἐντολῶν ἐκπληρώσεως, 5
ὅπως τῶν αἰωνίων καὶ ἀτελευτήτων ἀγαθῶν ἐπιτύχω-
μεν ἐν αὐτῷ Χριστῷ τῷ θεῷ ἡμῶν· ᾧ ἡ δόξα καὶ τὸ
κράτος εἰς τοὺς αἰῶνας τῶν αἰώνων· ἀμήν.]

NOTES.

THE TITLE.—For a full discussion of the title see p. 37 ff. It is there shown that the word Ἀναστάσιον, which occurs in V, did not originally form a part of the title, and it is therefore omitted in our edition.

P. 51, l. 9 ff. The incident here referred to by the Christian constituted a favorite argument for those who wrote in support of image worship. The passage in Genesis reads, in the A. V., "Israel bowed himself upon the bed's head." The Hebrew word translated *bed* is מטה, which means *bed* or *staff*, according as it is pointed מִטָּה or מַטֶּה. The LXX. chose the latter meaning, and translated προσεκύνησεν Ἰσραὴλ ἐπὶ τὸ ἄκρον τῆς ῥάβδου αὐτοῦ, which was followed exactly by the author of the Epistle to the Hebrews, xi. 21. In this form the passage was frequently quoted in support of image-worship, as, *e. g.*, by Psuedo-Athanasius in the extract quoted just below, and by Leontius in his discourse mentioned on p. 17. The Vulgate, meanwhile, translated the passage in the Epistle to the Hebrews *adoravit fastigium virgæ ejus*, giving quite a different turn to the sentence, and furnishing a still stronger argument for the worship of images, which Latin writers were not slow to take advantage of. Our dialogue likewise follows the Vulgate in making the ἄκρον τῆς ῥάβδου the direct object of προσεκύνησε.

P. 51, l. 14 ff. Compare the words of Pseudo-Athanasius in the *Quæstiones ad Antiochum ducem*, xxxix. (Migne, *Patr. Græc.*, xxviii. 621). The same line of argument is there presented. The incident in regard to Jacob, mentioned above, is reproduced in the following form: καὶ ὥσπερ Ἰακὼβ μέλλων τελευτᾷν ἐπὶ τὸ ἄκρον τῆς ῥάβδου τῷ Ἰωσὴφ προσεκύνησεν, οὐ τὴν ῥάβδον τιμῶν, ἀλλὰ τὸν ταύτην κατέχοντα κ.τ.λ. Compare also the discourse of Leontius mentioned in the previous note, also John of Damascus, *De fide orthodoxa*, iv. 11, and Gilbert's *Tractatus de incarnatione c. Judæos* (described on p. 23). The same argument occurs very frequently. Another still more common method was to show that even under the Jewish dispensation images were used and sanctioned by God, as, *e. g.*, the brazen serpent, the cherubim, etc. Still another way of meeting the Jews upon this subject appears in our dialogue, p. 75 ff. This introductory section upon image worship occurs in An., not at the beginning, but in the second treatise, in connection with the other passage just mentioned. The first tract of An. contains no reference to images.

P. 51, l. 23 ff. This shows the long standing of the practice. The passage from Pseudo-Athanasius referred to above makes the same statement.

P. 52, l. 3. The original dialogue begins at this point. In regard to the addition of the opening paragraph, see p. 37 ff.

P. 52, l. 6. This is a favorite passage with the authors of works against the Jews, but it is commonly employed in a different way; cf., *e. g.*, the use of the same text in the Dialogue of Simon and Theophilus, p. 19 (Harnack's *Texte und Untersuchungen*, Bd. I. Heft 3).

P. 52, l. 8. According to Theodoret (in his commentary on Daniel) this passage was applied by the Jews to Zerubbabel.

P. 52, l. 9. The agreement of An. with our dialogue commences at this point. It has two opening pages which are entirely wanting in P and V. It begins the present passage with the words εἰπὲ δὲ σὺ κ.τ.λ. Its mixed construction, sometimes direct discourse as in the present instance, sometimes indirect, clearly shows it to be a compilation, at whose basis lies an original of dialogistic form.

P. 52, l. 11. The form of the Jew's answer is significant. A real Jew would certainly have responded: "*At least* the half," etc., putting the emphasis upon the greatness of Solomon's kingdom, and not upon the smallness of it, as he is here represented as doing. This is but one of many marks of the artificial character of the dialogue.

P. 53, l. 1. The abrupt way in which the Jew passes on to a new subject, apparently quite satisfied with the Christian's answer, however meagre that answer may be, is a characteristic feature of the majority of these dialogues, and another mark of their artificial nature. The present dialogue is, however, extreme in this respect, for neither assent nor dissent is ever expressed by the Jew, who occupies, in fact, quite a passive position, and drops more and more into the background as the dialogue proceeds. Justin's Dialogue with Trypho, and Evagrius' Dialogue of Simon and Theophilus, are a deviation from the common rule, for in them the conclusions of the Christian are often disputed, and he is then obliged to ground them more firmly. This is a significant fact, for at the time when these dialogues were written (the Dial. of Simon and Theophilus being regarded as a reproduction of the Dial. of Papiscus and Jason) the Jew was an active factor who had to be reckoned with by Christian writers, and not a mere lay figure as he afterward became. It is natural, therefore, to find in the earlier works an honest effort to meet real objections which must have been raised by all Jews, as Jews. It would not be out of place to urge the fact, that the Dial. of Simon and Theophilus exhibits this characteristic, as an additional argument for Harnack's theory, that it is a reproduction of a much more ancient dialogue.

P. 53, l. 13. The epithet Θεοτόκος was very frequently applied to Mary by the Fathers of the fourth century (Eusebius, Athanasius, the two Gregories, etc.), and it was perhaps current in Alexandria in the third, though no absolute proof of this is at hand. It was officially adopted as an appellation of Mary at the Council of Ephesus (431), in opposition to Nestorius.

ἀεὶ παρθένου. The doctrine of the continued virginity of Mary is not older than Jerome. It appears in the Orient about as early as in the Occident. The same doctrine is discussed in the *Dial. of Simon and Theoph.*, in Gilbert's *Disputatio Judæi cum Christiano* (see p. 24), and in the anonymous *Tractatus adv. Judæos* (see p. 27). In the present instance, the words appear simply as part of a technical phrase long in current use.

It is possible, though only a possibility, that the words did not occur in the original Dialogue of Papiscus and Philo. They exist, to be sure, in all the extant witnesses, but they may have crept into the text through the unconscious error of a copyist, to whom the phrase had become so natural, in connection with the name of Mary, that he could scarcely avoid using it when writing the latter word. It is noticeable that in the present instance no emphasis is laid upon the virginity of Mary ; the point is simply that Christ was born of Mary, and the Jew takes it thus, and reveals no knowledge of the theological phrase introduced by the Christian, in which the miraculousness of the Saviour's birth is assumed. The Jew, it might seem, could hardly have passed such a claim by unnoticed, and indeed we find him objecting to it in the Dialogue of Theophilus and Simon, and in many of the later dialogues. Were our work the account of an actual dialogue between a Jew and a Christian, we should, therefore, be warranted in rejecting the words; but the artificial character of this and of other similar dialogues deprives the silence of the Jew of the significance which it would otherwise have. It remains therefore not a probability, but only a possibility, that these words were not a part of the original dialogue. The difference between the simple formula used here and the much fuller one used in P on p. 82 is very significant.

The passage, which occurs at this point in P, is omitted by V and An., and is clearly a later insertion of RP. It breaks the connection, and the answer of the Jew has relevancy only when taken in direct connection with Μαρίας, as it stands in V.

P. 54, l. 11. αὐτὸς τὸν υἱὸν κύριον ὁμολογεῖ. An. enlarges upon this subject, inserting almost half a page found neither in RV nor in RP.

P. 55, l. 14. Cf. Justin's *Dial. c. Trypho,* c. 34.

P. 56, l. 3. Cf. *ibid.* c. 49.

P. 56, l. 6. This external setting of the dialogue is, of course, omitted by An.

P. 56, l. 17 ff. This also.

P. 56, l. 22. The plural form, οἱ Ἰουδαῖοι, of P seems to have been caused by the reference to the crowd of Jews which has just preceded. The writer of RP apparently thinks of the audience as taking part in the discussion at this point, while RV confines it still to the single Jew.

P. 57, l. 10. This passage from Isaiah is quoted also on p. 66 in the section peculiar to P. It is given there in a somewhat different form, which shows clearly a different hand. In the *Testimonia* of Pseudo-Gregory the passage occurs in the form found here. It differs from Tischendorf's text of the LXX., in which Θαυμαστός and the following words are omitted. The Codex Alexandrinus, however, contains all except the word Θεός, and the Codex Sinaiticus contains the whole.

P. 57, l. 14. It is very significant that, in the passage inserted here by P, the phrase Θαυμαστός σύμβουλος is omitted, in agreement with the form of the quotation given on p. 66, and over against the form contained in V and An. The difference of authorship mentioned in the previous note is thus further confirmed.

P. 57, l. 15. The passage attributed here to Jeremiah is taken from the book of Baruch. The citation of this book under the name of Jeremiah was quite common. This same passage is referred to Jeremiah, for instance, by Cyprian in his *Testimonia*, by the Pseudo-Gregorian *Testimonia*, by Gregentius in his Dialogue with Herbanus, by Evagrius in the Dialogue of Simon and Theophilus, etc. In the work of Gilbert of Westminster (see above, p. 24) the passage is attributed by the Christian to Jeremiah, but the Jew denies Jeremiah's authorship, and calls the book of Baruch apocryphal. The Christian contends, on the other side, that the words were spoken by Jeremiah, and that Baruch took them down from his mouth.

P. 58, l. 6. It is noteworthy that Justin, in quoting this passage from the Psalms (Ps. xcv. 10), adds the apocryphal words ἀπό τοῦ ξύλου, and that Tertullian and Evagrius add the corresponding words *a ligno*.

P. 58, l. 7. The passage inserted here by P occurs neither in V nor in An. and is undoubtedly a later addition (cf. p. 31). The quotation from Malachi, however, occurs in a different part of An. in quite another connection, and there under the name of Isaiah.

P. 58, l. 12 ff. This passage (Gen xlix. 10) is very frequently quoted in works against the Jews, especially at a later period, when great stress was laid upon the misfortunes of the Jews over against the prosperity of the Christians.

P. 59, l. 10. These were the words of the High Priest, not of Christ.

P. 60, l. 5. According to tradition, St. Helena built a Christian church upon Mt. Sinai, and Justinian founded a monastery there two centuries later.

P. 60, l. 9 ff. Compare Theodoretus' *Comment. in Ezech.*, xlviii.: καὶ ἵνα τὰ ἄλια ἀντιλίπω μυρία ὄντα, ἔτι νῦν ἐν τοῖς Ἱεροσολύμοις, ἥτε τοῦ σταυροῦ ἐκκλησία, καὶ ἡ ἀνάστασις, καὶ ἡ ἀνάληψις, καὶ ἡ ἐν τῇ Ζιὼν ἐκκλησία, καὶ ἡ ἱερὰ Βηθλεέμ, καὶ ἕτεροι δὲ εὐκτήριοι τόποι μυρίοι." Compare also Gregentius' Dialogue with Herbanus, p. 602 (ed. Galland.).

P. 61, l. 9, note 84. The χιλίους χρόνους of P must be taken as a round number, for below (pp. 78 and 79) the author indicates that he is writing 1,000 years after the destruction of Jerusalem (see p. 42 ff.).

P. 61, l. 16. Upon the insertion of P at this point, as indicating the date of RP, see p. 43.

P. 61, l. 18. σφραγίς is used as *signum crucis* by Athanasius, Gregory Naz., and others. Cf. Chrysostom's *Homilia de adorat. S. crucis*, where the reason for this use of the word is given.

P. 62, l. 10. χρυσοῦν σταυρόν. Whether these words refer to a specific golden cross, or whether the term is used to indicate any cross which might be used in worship, I do not know. I have not found a parallel expression in any other work.

P. 64, l. 11. Such statements as this in regard to the Christians, when thrown into the present tense, seem to imply a hostile attitude of the surrounding world toward them; and this coincides with their actual position among the Mohammedans from the eighth century on. The statement cannot be insisted on in the present case as indicating peculiar hostility against the Christians in the home or at the period of the author, for the words may be used of the position of the Christians in general, or they may even be purely rhetorical and have reference only to the condition of the Christians in ancient times.

P. 65, l. 1. Upon the significance of these dates of V and An., see p. 42.

P. 65, l. 6. This is the only place in the dialogue where V has the plural Ἰουδαῖοι, and here P has the singular, which undoubtedly stood in the oldest form of the text. It is difficult to account for the plural form in this one place, when it occurs nowhere else; but it is possible that the long passage upon the affairs of the Jews in general, in which the Jews are addressed over and over again in the plural number, may have influenced the copyist of V, as the mention of the crowd of Jewish spectators influenced in one passage the copyist of P (see p. 87).

At this point begins the second tract of An.

P. 65, l. 17. At this point begin the greatest divergencies between RP and RV (see §§ 4 and 5 of the Introduction). Paragraph 12 is printed entire in the form given by V, and the same paragraph is then printed entire in the form given by P, the differences between the two forms being so great as to render any other method impracticable. The paragraph, which in V fills but sixteen lines, in P fills more than seven pages, beginning at p. 66, l. 8. An. contains only a part of the matter peculiar to P, and the form and arrangement of that common part is so different in the two works that it is impossible satisfactorily to indicate the parallels. The text of P is therefore given without variations.

P. 66, l. 14. Cf. the note upon this passage (Isa. ix. 6) on p. 88.

P. 66, l. 17. The use made of this passage (Isa. ix. 1-2) by our author is quite peculiar (cf. the interpretation of it given in Matt. iv. 14-16). He seems to have no idea of Palestinian geography, for he represents Christ as born in Bethlehem, and yet refers to the lands of Zebulun and Naphtali as the place of his birth. How he came to commit such a blunder, I do not know. The use made of the text in Matt. iv. 14-16, is quite different; so also in Cyprian's *Testimonia*. The text does not occur in Justin's Dialogue with Trypho, in Tertullian's *Adv. Judæos*, nor in the Dialogue of Simon and Theophilus.

P. 67, l. 27 ff. This passage is closely connected in subject with l. 12. The intervening sentences look like an insertion by a different hand. The passage moreover is omitted by An., which is another mark of the originality of the latter over against RP.

P. 68, l. 31. The passage quoted here (Ps. xl. 10) is referred to by almost all works of this kind as foretelling the betrayal of Christ by Judas, and is as a rule the only passage quoted as a prophecy of that act. But An. quite peculiarly omits it and quotes instead Ps. ii. 1-2, and interprets it as referring to the betrayal. The latter passage in P follows the other one, but is referred, not to the betrayal, but, as by all other writers, to the plots of the Jews, of Herod and of Pilate, against Christ.

P. 68, l. 34. Cf. Isidore's *Contra Judæos* (see p. 22), i. 19, 1 : "Quare fremuerunt gentes, id est Romani, et populi meditati sunt inania, hoc est Judæi ? Astiterunt reges terræ, hoc est Herodes et Pilatus, et principes convenerunt in unum, scilicet principes Sacerdotum et seniores Judæorum, adversus dominum et adversus Christum ejus."

P. 69, l. 8. The sudden change of construction here is peculiar (cf. the remarks on p. 37). It is the same form that occurs frequently in An., but happens to be omitted by it in this particular passage. It is probable therefore that the writer of RP had become familiar with the expression in using An., and inserted it here, in introducing a new subject, without thinking of its inconsistency with the dialogistic form of the rest of his work.

P. 69, l. 30. It is peculiar that this same form of appeal occurs in the *Demonstratio* of Hippolytus (see p. 14), chap. vii., but there in quite a different connection, as follows : διὰ τί, ὦ προφῆτα, εἰπὲ ἡμῖν, τίνος χάριν ὁ ναὸς ἠρημώθη; ἆρα διὰ τὴν πάλαι μοσχοποιίαν; ἆρα διὰ τὴν τοῦ λαοῦ εἰδωλολατρείαν ; ἆρα διὰ τὸ τῶν προφητῶν αἷμα; ἆρα διὰ τῆς μοιχείας καὶ πορνείας Ἰσραήλ ; οὐδαμῶς φησίν · κ.τ.λ. Aside from the opening phrase, this passage reminds us of p. 79 ff. of our dialogue. But there exist no other resemblances between our dialogue and the brief fragment of the *Demonstratio* known to us.

P. 70, l. 13. This quotation is from Zechariah and not from Jeremiah. Matthew also gives it as from Jeremiah, and that accounts for the error here, for the writer reproduces Matthew's text exactly at this point, and does not follow the LXX. The same error is committed by the author of the Dialogue of Gregentius with Herbanus, but the Pseudo-Greg. *Testimonia* correctly attribute the words to Zechariah.

P. 70, l. 17. The pretended site of the Potter's field is still shown (see Smith's Bible Dict., art. *Aceldama*).

P. 70, l. 20. It is peculiar that here the quotation, which is in the original prophecy in close connection with the preceding, should be correctly attributed to Zechariah. The ascription of the previous words to Jeremiah by Matthew was enough to make our author and others ascribe them to him, although they could not have quoted these words from Zechariah, as they do quote them, without seeing that the other words were but a part of the same passage. The incident shows how slavishly the New Testament was followed.

P. 70, l. 27 ff. The writer here takes liberties with the text in omitting the word "Solomon," which occurs in the original.

P. 70, l. 38 ff. Cf. John Dam., *de fide orthod.* iv. 11.

P. 72, l. 27. P quotes this passage (Zech. xii. 10) exactly in the form given in Theodotion's version of the Old Testament, which differs from the form given in the LXX., and also from that given in John xix. 37, where the passage is quoted.

P. 74, l. 4. For the bearing of these sentences upon the question as to the home of our dialogue, see p. 43 ff. All the cults mentioned point to Egypt, except those of Cyzicus and of Artemis, which point to Asia Minor (cf. Pliny, xxxvi. 15, where the temple of Cyzicus is mentioned).

P. 75, l. 16. This passage occurs in An. in the same connection, but has joined with it the opening paragraph of our dialogue. The combination in An. is clearly later than the separation in P and V. For the combination of the two detached passages, the reason is plain enough, but their separation, if they were originally one, would be inexplicable.

P. 76, l. 3 ff. This section is very similar to passages in many later works against the Jews, nearly all of which devote considerable space to the blindness and wickedness of the Jews in the face of all God's providences. Compare also Justin's Dialogue with Trypho, c. 131.

P. 76, l. 12 ff. See Ex. iv. 16; vii. 1; xviii. 19.

P. 78, l. 13 ff. Cf. II. Kings, xxi.

P. 78, l. 24. On this date see p. 42.

P. 79, l. 7. As was shown on p. 42, it is probable that πεντακόσια should be read here instead of ἑξακόσια. I have not, however, cared to introduce a conjectural emendation into the text, and have therefore allowed the suspected word to stand.

P. 79, l. 13 ff. Cf. the quotation from the work of Hippolytus given on p. 90.

P. 80, l. 2 ff. In the work of Thaddæus Pelusiota against the Jews (see p. 18), this sentence occurs word for word, and the whole line of thought of the context is similar. The resemblance is so great as to necessitate some sort of literary relationship, but what that may be I am not prepared to state. I have noticed no other striking resemblance between the two works.

P. 80, l. 20. The dialogue as given in V comes to an end at this point, as also the second tract of An. The third tract of An. contains scattering points of resemblance to P in connection with the prophetic details of Christ's life, as mentioned on p. 36. Otherwise it is quite different from P, containing a mass of material not found in the latter.

P. 81, l. 30 ff. The simplicity of this confession of faith is noteworthy at so late a date. Compare what is said on the subject in § 1. Cf. also Justin's Dialogue with Trypho, c. 34, 85, 126, 132.

P. 82, l. 25. The quotation resembles the text of Matthew more closely than that of Daniel, but differs from both, and from all the parallel passages in the Gospels, in substituting $\theta\epsilon o\tilde{v}$ for $\dot{\alpha}\nu\theta\rho\dot{\omega}\pi o\nu$.

P. 82, l. 27. The author allows himself some license here in substituting for the $\dot{\alpha}\sigma\epsilon\beta\eta$ of Isaiah an $\alpha\dot{v}\tau\dot{o}\nu$ referring to the Antichrist. He evidently quotes from memory, and as a consequence quotes the passage from Isaiah (if this is the passage he intends to quote, and I can refer his words to no other) inexactly.

P. 82, l. 30 ff. These words are very significant, as showing that the intention of the work was to confirm the faith of the Christians rather than to refute the Jews (see p. 3).

P. 82, l. 36 ff. Compare the heaped-up epithets of Mary with the much simpler formula on p. 53.

SCRIPTURE REFERENCES.

	PAGE
Gen. xiv. 18 sq	55
xlvii. 31	51
xlix. 10	58
Ex. xxxii. 4	75
Deut. xxviii. 66	72
xxxii. 5-6	77
" 6	77
" 15	78
" 17	78
" 20	77
Job ix. 8	67
xiv. 4-5	69
xxxviii. 17	73
Psa. ii. 1-2	68
" 7	52
" 7-9	52
" 8	66
viii. 2-3	68
xv. 10	73
xvii. 10	65, 66
" 11	73
xxi. 17	65
" 17-18	71
" 19	65, 71
xxviii. 3	67
xxxiv. 11-12	69
xxxvii. 18	70
xl. 10	68
xlvi. 1	58, 66
" 6	73
" 9	58, 66
lxvii. 7	73
lxviii. 22	65, 72
" 23-24	72
lxxi. 1	55
" 5	55
" 6	66
" 7-8	67

	PAGE
Psa. lxxi. 8	55
" 11	67
" 17	55, 67
lxxiii. 12	71
" 13-14	67
lxxvii. 20	77
" 21	77
" 30-31	77
lxxxv. 9	66, 68
" 9-10	58
lxxxvi. 5	67
lxxxvii. 5-6	73
" 7	73
xcv. 10	58
xcvii. 5	58
cix. 1	54
" 3	54
" 4	54
cxvii. 26	56, 57
" 27	56
cxlii. 2	69
Prov. viii. 24-25	53, 55
Cant. iii. 11	70
Isa. i. 2-4	77
" 10	78
iii. 9-10	69
" 10	68
vii. 14	65, 66
ix. 1-2	66
" 6	57, 66, 70
xi. 4	82
xix. 1	67
xxvii. 11	73
l. 6	70
liii. 1	68
" 4	67
" 7	69
" 8	69

	PAGE		PAGE
Isa. liii. 9	69	Zech. xii. 10	72
" 12	71	xiii. 6	71
lvii. 1	72	xiv. 4	73
" 1-2	72	" 6-7	72
lxiii. 9	66	" 8	72
Jer. v. 21	62	Mal. i. 10-11	58
Dan. vii. 9-10	82	Baruch iii. 36-38	57
" 11	82	Hymn of the Three Holy Children,	
" 13	82	verse 14	60
" 13-14	81	Matt. vi. 1	64
" 15	82	x. 18	66
ix. 23-24	81	xvi. 18	63
" 26	81	xxiv. 2	59, 63
" 27	81, 82	" 30	82
Hos. ii. 23	58	xxviii. 19	64
vi. 1-2	66, 73	" 20	64
Joel iii. 15	72	Mark xiv. 22	64
Amos viii. 9	72	xvi. 15	63
Mic. v. 2	66	Luke xiv. 26	64
Hab. i. 5	72	xxi. 17	63
iii. 3	57	John i. 29	70
Zech. ix. 9	68	xi. 48	59
xi. 12	70	II. Tim. ii. 19	63
" 12-13	70